D1608693

Boxes

THE SMITHSONIAN ILLUSTRATED LIBRARY OF ANTIQUES

General Editor: Nancy Akre

Boxes

William C. Ketchum, Jr.

COOPER-HEWITT MUSEUM

The Smithsonian Institution's National Museum of Design

ENDPAPERS

Selection of American bandboxes, c. 1820–45. Cooper-Hewitt Museum, gifts of Eleanor and Sarah Hewitt and Mrs. F. F. Thompson

FRONTISPIECE

Inro, five sections, black lacquer and gold on wood decorated with lead, pottery, mother-of-pearl and tortoiseshell. Although inro were a common element of Japanese dress, they received the careful attention of skilled artists. Japanese, signed No-gakuhei, late eighteenth century. Length: 11 cm. (4 in.). Metropolitan Museum of Art, New York, bequest of Edward C. Moore, 1891

Printed in the United States of America
Library of Congress Catalog Card Number: 82–72760

Art Direction, Design: Joseph B. Del Valle

Picture Editor: Dorothy Sinha

Contents

1 Introduction

Stated most simply, boxes are usually just covered containers. In the history of mankind, however, they have represented a great deal more than that. Often the function of boxes has been less important than the social role they have played. Ritual containers to house everything from food to perfumes have been found in ancient Egyptian and Chinese tombs. Medieval boxes might also have a religious role, some of the finest examples being those made to honor Christian relics such as saints' bones. Other containers were intended for jewelry and perfumes. During the seventeenth and eighteenth centuries the European snuffbox became a mark of social distinction, accepted as a gift from royalty or carried as a symbol of social position. And the nineteenth-century Indians of the Northwest Coast of North America carved remarkably sophisticated wooden boxes in which to store the gifts offered at their potlatches, or ritual exchanges of presents.

It is hardly surprising that boxes come in a remarkable variety of shapes, sizes and materials. Some, like the *pillbox*, are tiny; others like the *tea caddy* or Japanese "picnic" box, may be large enough to make us wonder whether they should be called boxes at all since they more closely resemble chests or trunks. The variations in shape may merely reflect stylistic preference but are more likely to reflect function. A thin, flat cigarette or visiting-card case is immediately recognizable in terms of its use; so, inside, is the carefully compartmented sewing box. Yet other containers, such as snuffs and *nécessaires*, come in a plethora of forms, many of which quite effectively mask the object's true function.

The materials used to make boxes vary just as widely. Early examples were carved from wood or stone or made of baked clay. Those materials, although they have continued to be used—particularly in

Colorplate 1.
Cosmetic box, wood embellished with gold and enamelwork. This container was once filled with elaborate toilet articles similar to the ones illustrated. Egyptian, Twelfth Dynasty (c. 2000–1786 B.C.). Height: 37.5 cm. (14¾ in.). Metropolitan Museum of Art, New York

less advanced cultures and in the folk art of more highly developed nations—were soon joined by a host of other, sometimes exotic, mediums.

Precious metals, especially silver, have long been popular for boxmaking. The white metal was very suitable for snuffboxes as it could most easily be *engraved* with the appropriate inscriptions. Finer pieces were made of gold or platinum and might be covered with precious gems.

Larger containers were made of other metals. Bronze and later brass and *pewter* were popular in China and Southeast Asia; iron, elaborately shaped and decorated, found favor in medieval Europe. Brass, copper, tin (both plain and *japanned*) and Britannia metal were all used on the Continent. Often, metals were combined; particularly common were examples in brass and copper or in brass and iron.

The tiny Japanese *inro*—compartmented boxes used to carry seals, medicines or other objects (frontispiece)—were sometimes carved out of nuts, although ivory or jade was generally preferred. Semiprecious stones such as garnet and sodalite were used, too. In the nineteenth century, tea caddies and card cases made of tortoiseshell were so common as to endanger the existence of the great tortoises. Seashells like abalone and cowrie were more fragile but sometimes favored for snuff mulls and perfume containers. Other unusual materials include horn, papier-mâché, shagreen and *straw-work*, the last featuring complex geometric and pictorial surfaces achieved by glueing split straw to paper.

The more traditional materials were of course modified to suit changing tastes. Wood was elaborately *inlaid* with contrasting timbers or strips of metal, or was covered with *lacquer*, a technique especially common in the Orient. The simple earthenware containers of an earlier era were replaced by finely painted porcelain examples, and the ancient technique of *cloisonné*, involving the application of enamels to a metal base, was utilized to produce a variety of delicate and jewel-like containers.

The making of such boxes obviously took up a great deal of time and needed no small amount of experience. Many were works of art, and almost all were produced one at a time. But during the nineteenth century, especially in the Western world, boxmaking became industrialized. Boxes were needed for many practical purposes and in large quantities; new techniques of manufacture inevitably developed.

Small boxes had been cast of iron or lead for centuries. Most of these were trinket or *tobacco boxes*, and the weight of the material limited the practical use of this fast and efficient casting method. However, the development of tin (thin sheet iron covered with tinplate to prevent rust) and the subsequent invention of lithography revolutionized the world of boxes. From the early 1800s on, large numbers of shop- and factory-made boxes started to appear. These were used chiefly for storage and to transport foodstuffs and other commercial products, proving both light in weight and surprisingly durable. Equally important, such containers could provide a means of advertising. Decorated with bright chromolithographed messages, tobacco, biscuit and soap boxes proclaimed their products throughout the Western world.

Today, particularly in the United States, tin boxes dating from the late nineteenth and early twentieth centuries are avidly collected. Of somewhat lesser interest, primarily due to their fragility, are the paper and cardboard boxes with equally attractive lithographed surfaces. These, too, have been around for almost two centuries. Small circular French *comfit boxes* for candied fruits were being made soon after 1800, and by 1900 cardboard boxes for anything from crackers to shirtwaists were a common sight on grocery and dry-goods store shelves. Since they were mass-produced, such containers are still readily available to collectors.

The designs of these boxes are rewarding to the art historian and the collector for their own merits, of course, but also because they often mirror in miniature the stylistic developments prevailing during the age in which they were created. It is possible to find Renaissance, rococo or Art Deco boxes, each a reflection of the architecture, furniture and larger decorative accessories of its time.

But it is impossible, finally, to lose sight of function. Some boxes were indeed almost entirely decorative in purpose; others, such as the snuff- and pillboxes, were certainly more ornate than their purpose would seem to dictate. Yet a huge array of simple pieces also exists whose form and decoration clearly mirror and complement their purpose. Among the best examples are the American Shaker containers and the innumerable household boxes (both Eastern and Western) to hold everything from spices and candies to linens, knives or money. Practicality was the rule with their creators, and the boxes did their job well.

Unlike those antiques that have largely vanished along with the needs that led to their creation, boxes continue to be made in many shapes, sizes and materials. Some are decorative; most are practical. All undoubtedly serve in some way to enhance our lives.

2 The Earliest Boxes

Given the obvious importance of containers in every culture, one might assume that boxes existed in quantity at the earliest periods, even though time and the ravages of history must have taken their toll. In fact, excavations at the sites of ancient cities and burial grounds have generally yielded few clues to the types of containers once used in local cultures. There are, however, certain happy exceptions. One of the most prominent is in Egypt, where the custom of entombing a person of rank with many of his belongings resulted in the preservation of a wide variety of box types.

Perhaps the greatest of these finds have come from the Nile Valley of the Kings, where many of the ancient Egyptian pharaohs were buried; and best known of all the treasures are those from the tomb of Tutankhamun, the young ruler of the late Eighteenth Dynasty (reigned c. 1334–1325 B.C.). By a series of fortuitous circumstances, this pharaoh's tomb was not discovered and ravaged by grave robbers. When opened by modern scholars in 1922, it was found to be almost intact, and included among the artifacts were a large number of boxes.

These containers reveal the Egyptians as remarkable craftsmen who were capable of creating very diverse boxes in different materials. The shapes varied greatly: square or rectangular *coffers* with tops flat or domed; curved boxes to hold bows, and high arching ones for ceremonial hats. There is even a peculiar double box in the form of the royal cartouche, sheathed with gold inset with a multitude of glass beads, one of the earliest versions of paste jewels.

The sophistication of these pieces came as a shock to the modern eye. Complex and well-stocked cosmetic boxes (colorplate 1) consist of precious woods such as ebony and cedar, inlaid with ivory or lapis lazuli and encrusted with semiprecious stones. Cylindrical containers for unguents are mounted upon feet carved in the shape of

Colorplate 2.
Game box, blue- and black-glazed faience. The Egyptians played various games similar to chess or checkers, and this box and counters would have been used for one of them. Egyptian, Late Eighteenth Dynasty (c. 1570–1293 B.C.). Length: 21 cm. (8¼ in.). Brooklyn Museum, New York, The Charles Edwin Wilbour Fund

African or Asian heads. Chests for storing clothing or textiles come meticulously painted with scenes depicting important battles or royal hunts.

Some of these containers are of solid gold or carved alabaster, but the great majority are simply of wood or even woven reed. Reed, after all, was easily obtainable along the Nile and certainly inexpensive; one suspects that most containers used by the common people would probably have been made of it.

The boxes found in the dynastic tombs tell us a great deal about life in pharaonic Egypt. We know that cosmetics were used, that games were played (colorplate 2), that dressing boxes often came equipped with mirrors, and that the hieroglyphs written on the tops and sides of containers might be prayers to the gods or simply a statement of what was inside. Egyptian boxes are surprisingly revealing about their culture.

Unfortunately, not all cultures have left so clear a record. There are fragments, though, that give a tantalizing glimpse of what was once available in comparable societies. From Sumeria, about 2500 B.C., come the treasures of Ur. They include a cedar box covered with gold leaf, inlaid with mother-of-pearl and lapis lazuli in a skillful design illustrating a king's triumph, complete with the victorious ruler and his court, marching troops, prisoners and a variety of booty. Other Sumerian containers are of ebony, gold or alabaster, and may be intricately decorated.

At a later date, although in the same general area, the artisans of the great Assyrian Empire (c. 1115–612 B.C.) produced remarkably carved ivory boxes. Gold and bronze were worked into receptacles in many parts of Europe and the Near East, most notably in those lands held by the Etruscans (plate 1).

Pottery, too, was a popular boxmaking medium, perhaps exceeded only by wood. As early as 2500 B.C., terra-cotta boxes were being made in the Indus Valley area of India, while the Minoan (c. 3000–1100 B.C.) and the Mycenaean (c. 1400–1100 B.C.) cultures turned out a number of different containers, most intended for purposes we can only guess at.

The ceramic arts in the Aegean reached their zenith with the so-called Classical period, during much of which Athens was the dominant state. Around 600 B.C. Greek artisans began to produce a high-quality earthenware characterized by figure decoration painted freehand in black on a background that might be tan, yellow or a shade of red. Soon after 500 B.C. the color scheme but not the decoration was altered, so that figures in red now appeared on a light tan or black ground (colorplate 3). These figures are at once lively and naturalistic, and the scenes include merchants, athletes and soldiers. Consequently, black and red figure ware is important not only for its inherent beauty but as a documentary trace of a long-lost civilization.

1

1.
Toilet box (pyxis), silver inlaid with gold. The ability to work precious metals was well developed in the eastern Mediterranean long before the time of Christ. Etruscan, fourth to third century B.C. Height: 8.4 cm. (3¼ in.). Metropolitan Museum of Art, New York, Rogers Fund, 1903

2.
Toilet box (pyxis), carved ivory. This container is typical of the smaller pieces made by Roman craftsmen, who often decorated their wares with pagan figures such as this satyr prior to the spread of Christianity. Roman, first century A.D. Height: 5 cm. (2 in.). Metropolitan Museum of Art, New York, Rogers Fund, 1923

2

Ceramic boxes may be circular, like the one pictured here, or less commonly square or rectangular. Greek containers are also found in other mediums, particularly silver, gold and bronze. In most cases the original function of the pieces is now lost, although we know that some were for cosmetics, unguents and perfumes, and larger examples appear to have been designed for the storage of food.

As befits the rulers of the world's most practical early empire, the Romans found uses for a large number of containers. Wall paintings unearthed in their ancient cities show citizens handling and using everything from delicate perfume and toilet boxes to large storage chests and trunks. These they produced in many shapes and forms, with flat, domed or peaked tops; choice examples might be made from precious imported woods such as ebony or from solid gold or silver.

The surface decoration of the Roman containers varied just as much. Some were simply painted in one or two solid colors, or covered with leather; others might bear illustrations from the ancient myths, either carved or painted on the sides and cover. Carved decoration was especially common on the small boxes, known as *pyxides*, which were used in ancient Greece and Rome to store salves and toiletries. Often they were made from alabaster or ivory (plate 2).

These boxes reflect the gradual ascendance of Christianity throughout the empire. At first they were embellished with such popular deities as Pan and Bacchus; then, in time, they came to be ornamented instead with depictions of martyrs and the Trinity.

The decoration and the design of Greek and Roman boxes are also important for their influence on similar containers made at a much later date. Europe was always fascinated by the Classical era, and from the Renaissance right down to the Classical revival in the eighteenth century, designers would base their creations—whether boxes or furniture—on their perceptions of the Greek or Roman style.

Colorplate 3.
Toilet box (pyxis), earthenware decorated with paint. This Greek pyxis, found at Cumae on the Italian Peninsula, depicts a scene from the Judgment of Paris. Athenian, Greek, c. 470 B.C. Height: 14.6 cm. (5¾ in.). Metropolitan Museum of Art, New York, Rogers Fund, 1907

3 English and Continental Boxes

When enthusiasts speak of box collecting, they are often referring to the acquisition and display of containers made in the British Isles and on the Continent, for without doubt an enormous number and variety of boxes have been produced in these areas. Based on a tradition extending back to Greek and Roman times, master craftsmen have turned out boxes in every conceivable form and of almost every imaginable material over the centuries. Available examples range from the half-inch pill- and *patch boxes* to surprisingly large sewing and storage boxes. Most of these objects date from the eighteenth to the twentieth century. Earlier examples may occasionally be found but are now generally housed in public collections.

One might assume that most of these containers were simply intended to hold something; after all, that is the primary purpose of a box. Yet such are the vagaries of human nature that many English and European boxes—especially the most attractive and therefore most collectible—served other functions. They were intended as gifts; as tokens of social or political status; as mementos of loved ones; and, of course, as souvenirs of places visited or special events. A person attending the coronation of the aging Edward VII in London, for example, could purchase an enamel comfit box (plate 3) in memory of the occasion (comfits being small bits of fruit, nuts or seeds preserved in sugar). In many instances, such pieces would not bear any particular mark to associate them with the momentous event, although perhaps the most interesting to the collector are those that are labeled (plate 4).

Boxes in England The practice of bestowing boxes as gifts or mementos has a long and illustrious history in the British Isles. Queen

Colorplate 4.
Small box in the form of a spaniel resting on a cushion, enamel on copper with brass hinges. The affable black-and-white spaniel has long held a special place in the hearts of English artists and craftsmen, although never more so than in the eighteenth century. English, c. 1770. Height: 3.8 cm. (1½ in.). Cooper-Hewitt Museum, bequest of Katherine Strong Welman

3.
Comfit box, enamel over base metal with gilt edging. This container was one of many souvenirs prepared as part of the festivities connected with the coronation of Edward VII in London. English, 1902. Width: 9.5 cm. (3¾ in.). Cooper-Hewitt Museum, gift of Mr. Dreyfous du Moulin

4.
Interior of the above comfit box, showing the royal cartouche and the label CORONATION SOUVENIR.

5.
Interior view of box with two compartments, enamel on copper with gilt-metal mounts. Humorous paintings of animals mimicking human behavior were popular in the eighteenth century. English, probably Bilston, Staffordshire, eighteenth century. Width: 7.5 cm. (3 in.). Cooper-Hewitt Museum, bequest of Sarah Cooper Hewitt

Elizabeth I (1533–1603) is recorded as having received a small oaken coffer or chest from an admirer. Carved, gilded and painted, it was filled with silver combs and perfume bottles, and even equipped with a mirror.

Wood Such wooden containers were among the earliest made in England. The few remaining fifteenth- and sixteenth-century specimens show heavy carving; at a slightly later date, there is additional painted decoration in what were once bright colors. Changes in taste and developments in craftsmanship led to seventeenth-century *marquetry* boxes whose entire surfaces were covered with geometric or floral pattern inlays in contrasting woods.

The steam-driven turning and carving machines perfected during the nineteenth century resulted in a vast proliferation of wooden boxes. These were sold as souvenirs, but were also used as storage places by men to hold their coins, cuff links and collar studs; by women for their various cosmetics, soaps and hair preparations; and in the pantry or in the kitchen to hold salt, matches and many other items.

The so-called *Tunbridge ware*, largely handmade at the popular spa of Tunbridge Wells in Kent, was established by the end of the seventeenth century and retained its popularity into the 1890s. Unlike most earlier boxes, these wooden mosaic souvenir pieces were specifically designed to be sold inexpensively in large quantities. At first the mosaic decoration was abstract; but later quite detailed portraits of well-known figures and views of local points of interest were created by glueing together rods of different-colored wood, then cutting these into thin strips for application to the tops and sides of the boxes. In the 1850s and 1860s the tiny pictures of cathedrals, castles and stately homes were intended to appeal to a class of buyers who for the first time could afford to travel and even to spend a bit for something to remind them of the trip. Today, Tunbridge ware, also known as "English mosaics," is much prized.

Less expensive to produce were small round, square or rectangular wooden boxes decorated with transfer-printed scenes. Done from copper plates, most often in black, these pieces were frequently dated and labeled with their locality, which renders them particularly collectible.

A third category of inexpensive souvenirs is known as Mauchline ware. These wooden receptacles included pill-, trinket and stamp boxes, as well as needle- and seal cases. One type of Mauchline ware is decorated with transfer-printed portraits and views of historic sites, while another is embellished with bits of paper on which were printed the tartans of the various Scottish clans. Yet a third type is composed of the small round stamp boxes in which uncut postage stamps of the period 1840 to 1854 were stored. The choicest of these containers will have an original "Penny Red" stamp inset into the lid.

4

Enamels Among the finest of English containers are those of painted *enamel*. It is generally agreed that the pride of English enamels are the so-called *Battersea boxes*, produced very briefly at York House in Battersea during the mid-eighteenth century. Later factories at Bilston and Wednesbury in Staffordshire also turned out high-quality pieces. The painted decoration on these varies greatly. In a serious vein, there are historical landscapes, portraits of important personages and re-creations of great battles. But more often the topic is humorous, the surfaces being decorated with paintings of animals, sometimes depicted in human guise (plate 5).

Because enameling proved difficult on the larger areas of containers designed to hold such items as knives, tobacco or tea, it was primarily reserved for small objects. Chief among these are the small containers in which snuff—a preparation of ground and sometimes perfumed tobacco—was stored. Tobacco was seen growing in Haiti by members of Columbus's crew, and within a few years it was being used in Spain as an herbal remedy. However, it was not until the seventeenth century that use of tobacco spread generally through western Europe. The snuffbox was devised to store the pulverized tobacco, which was taken primarily by inhaling through the nose.

Enameling was also common on *patch boxes* (see page 22), comfit boxes and *étuis*—the last being complex little cases that could be popped into a pocket or hung on a chatelaine, which were used by women to hold their toilet or sewing articles. All these containers were normally round, oval or square, but they might also appear as

5

6

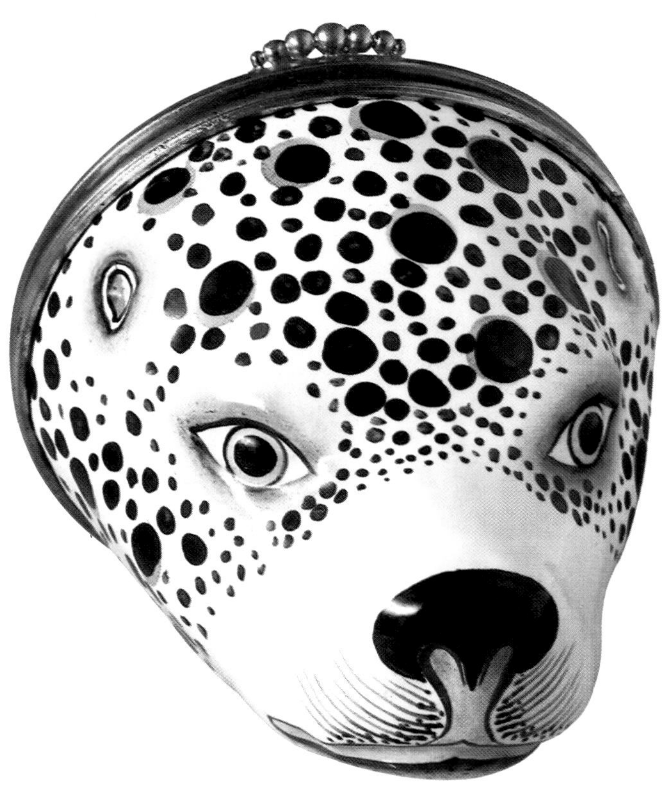

Colorplate 5.
Novelty box in the form of a dog's head. This enamel-on-copper box has gilt-metal mounts and was probably intended to hold candies or pills. English, c. 1850. Diameter: 5.5 cm. (2¼ in.). Cooper-Hewitt Museum, gift of Sarah Cooper Hewitt

6.
Box in the shape of a sparrow, enamel on copper. Small boxes in the form of birds or animals were often given as gifts to loved ones. English, South Staffordshire, c. 1770. Length: 6.6 cm. (2⅝ in.). Cooper-Hewitt Museum, bequest of Katherine Strong Welman

7.
Shell-shaped sugar or spice box, silver. In the seventeenth century sugar and spices were precious rarities quite worthy of the finest silver containers. English, c. 1621–22. Length: 12.7 cm. (5 in.). Minneapolis Institute of Arts, James F. Bell Memorial Fund

birds (plate 6), dogs (colorplate 4) or even in the shape of a Dalmatian's head (colorplate 5). Their charm is self-evident, and they have won a permanent place in the hearts of collectors. (Unfortunately this popularity has led over the years to many reproductions, both English and Continental.)

Silver English silver is of course famous all over the world. Much of the early silversmiths' work was melted down during the Reformation, so that few of their containers remain outside the museums and universities. But literary references indicate that silver boxes had long been popular. Early in the seventeenth century, craftsmen devised the ornate shell-shaped spice or sugar box to grace an upper-class pantry or dining room (plate 7); and among the most traditional pieces in the current baroque manner were bridal toilet services for women, sometimes consisting of as many as twenty matching pieces, which would include several boxes and small caskets. Toilet cases—also known as dressing boxes—were used just as heavily by men to hold a large array of toilet articles and accessories.

Sugar, spice and toilet boxes of silver continued to be made during the eighteenth century, while the prevailing style, the rococo, manifested itself in the equipment required for drinking tea, already popular in the British Isles. The tea caddy was a tightly sealed container used to preserve and protect tea, since the leaves were quite valuable and hard to come by when they first appeared in Europe. Tea caddies usually had two compartments, one for green and one for black tea; often a lock was fitted to discourage pilfering. Elaborately wrought silver tea caddies provide one of the best examples of English craftsmanship (plate 8).

Among the finest examples of the smaller early pieces made by

7

silversmiths were the *vinaigrettes.* These tiny containers had hinged lids and inner perforated covers beneath which a small sponge saturated with aromatic vinegar was concealed. Women overcome with faintness or assaulted by the unpleasant odors so common everywhere could revive themselves by sniffing this concoction. Vinaigrettes appeared in diverse shapes, sometimes disguised as watches, books, purses or eggs.

Other pieces of eighteenth- and nineteenth-century silver included snuffboxes that might be *embossed*, engraved or covered with bright-cut decoration; pill and nutmeg containers; and the shallower receptacles known as patch boxes, which held tiny pieces of taffeta or silk that were applied to the face. Although often referred to as "beauty spots," patches were frequently used (by both sexes) to conceal the unsightly scars left by smallpox. The later patch boxes were elaborately designed to hold different patches and even a pot of gum with accompanying brush.

During the nineteenth century the types of containers manufactured by English silversmiths continued to increase. The introduction in the 1740s of Sheffield plate (produced by a plating process in which silver is fused to copper), followed by electroplated silver, which was produced by immersing a piece of copper or pewter in an electrolytic solution containing silver in suspension, then passing an electric charge through it, meant that a much wider range of pieces could be produced for a larger clientele. Adopted from France, the widespread Victorian custom of leaving visiting cards led to the production of many types of card cases. Snuffboxes declined in

8.
Three tea caddies, silver. The introduction of tea from the Orient led to the production of elaborate containers to hold the very popular but expensive tea leaves. English, by William Vincent, c. 1768–69. Height of tallest: 14.5 cm. (5¾ in.). Minneapolis Institute of Arts, gift of the Charles Bolles Rogers family

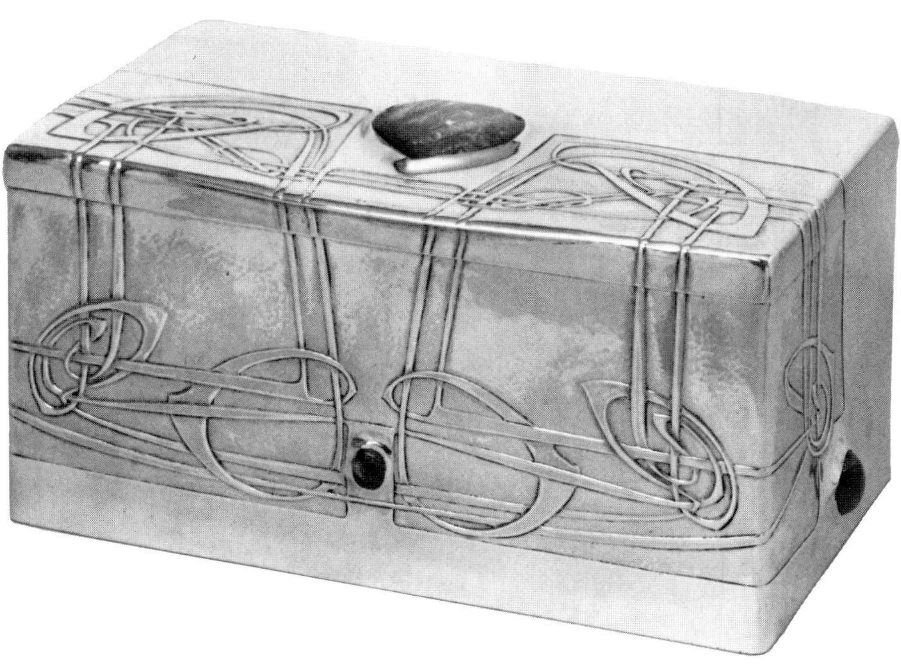

9.
Casket, silver over a wooden base set with opal matrix. This charming piece is typical of the English wares in the "Liberty" style that influenced Continental and American design. English, Liberty & Company, London, 1903. Length: 21.6 cm. (8½ in.). Victoria and Albert Museum

popularity as the habit of taking snuff dwindled, but the new craze for smoking fostered the development of cigar and cigarette cases and matchsafes. Dresser sets with their many powder and perfume containers proliferated, and countless small trinket or jewelry boxes were produced. The former, usually less elaborate and costly than jewel boxes, were used to house a lady's ribbons, buckles, necklaces and pins.

As befits the eclecticism of the period, most such pieces were in one of the current revival styles or, more often, a variety of styles forced into a somewhat unnatural marriage. However, by the mid-nineteenth century English designers were growing weary of traditional Victorian silver and began developing new ideas. Out of this ferment emerged, first, the Arts and Crafts movement, and later the British version of Art Nouveau.

Arts and Crafts–style silver was made in limited quantity and so is hard to find. But the late-nineteenth- to early-twentieth-century metalwork boxes and caskets produced by Liberty & Company of London are a fine example of Art Nouveau (plate 9). So typical of the mode are their flowing lines and whiplike decorative motifs that the Italians dubbed Art Nouveau the "stile Liberty."

Other Metals Iron, tin, brass, copper, pewter and even lead were used for more workaday containers. In the seventeenth century, when snuff taking became so popular, British craftsmen were already turning out tin-plated sheet-iron snuffboxes that were *japanned*, a process that involved painting the surface with many layers of color and clear varnish. This technique was soon applied to tin pieces, and by the nineteenth century English *toleware* (painted tin) boxes were being manufactured in industrial centers and distributed by traders throughout much of the world.

Brass and copper were used in the making of eighteenth- and nineteenth-century engine-turned snuff-, spice, and tobacco boxes. The Lancaster snuffs were particularly ingenious, their keyless locks representing a forerunner of the modern combination lock: when the pointers on two clocklike dials were set at a certain combination of numbers, the box would open smoothly.

Matchsafes, the small, watertight containers in which friction matches were stored, were often made of brass and copper. While the earliest of these were simply boxes, by the late nineteenth century they had assumed a diversity of forms, including such improbable examples as basketballs, dominoes and violins. One major seller of matchsafes was Bryant & May of London, who offered containers representing notable figures: Queen Victoria, Bismarck and Christopher Columbus, among others.

Some early matchsafes, known as Vesta boxes, were shaped like small books. The top side, corresponding to a book's binding, opened to provide access to the matches; a serrated edge provided a friction surface. The later boxes, in numerous shapes (colorplate 6), had openings at one end. The more expensive metal containers generally had an inner surface plated with gold to avoid corrosion by the sulphur.

Today, matchsafes are great favorites with collectors in England and abroad. Examples incorporating other tools or objects—toothpicks, penknives, candleholders and stamp and coin holders—are particularly sought after.

Pewter boxes generally followed the style of those in silver. They were practical for storing tinder, cigarettes and cigars and were used by ladies for trinkets and a variety of table and toilet purposes. Less often found are the heavy lead tobacco containers cast during the Georgian and Victorian eras. These were sometimes painted, and with the passage of time may appear to be much older than they actually are.

Colorplate 6.
Matchsafe in the form of an early basketball, with hinged top and loop for attaching a chain. The fanciful shapes of matchboxes have long made them great favorites with collectors. English, late nineteenth to early twentieth century. Diameter: 5.7 cm. (2¼ in.). Cooper-Hewitt Museum, gift of Carol B. Brener and Stephen W. Brener

Natural Materials Natural materials were popular, especially for small and delicate receptacles. During the eighteenth and early nineteenth centuries snuffboxes were often made of tortoiseshell, bound in gold and decorated with miniature watercolor or enamel portraits of their owner, a member of his family or the donor of the box (plate 10). Snuff- and patch boxes and even étuis were sometimes constructed out of seashells, particularly cowrie and mussel (plate 11), which would be given silver linings and clasps.

10.
Snuffbox, tortoiseshell with gold mounts and an enamel miniature portrait. In the eighteenth century snuffboxes bearing a portrait of the donor were often given as gifts. English, c. 1770–79. Length: 7.8 cm. (3 in.). Cooper-Hewitt Museum, bequest of Sarah Cooper Hewitt

11.
Three snuffboxes made from seashells mounted in silver. Snuffs of cowrie, mussel and other shells were once common; but most are unmarked and their locality is now hard to identify. English or Continental, eighteenth to nineteenth century. Length of cowrie box: 7.9 cm. (3⅛ in.). Cooper-Hewitt Museum, center shell, gift of Susan Dwight Bliss; top and bottom shells, gift of Sarah Cooper Hewitt

In the late nineteenth and early twentieth centuries shells were used to make the small souvenir boxes widely sold at English coastal resorts. Frequently rather flimsy in nature, these containers were created by glueing groups of small shells to a cardboard or wooden box to create interesting decorative effects.

Shells are also found on the English sewing, or *workboxes*, which can often be discovered complete with date and place name. The shells for these did not come from the British Isles but were imported from Asia, Africa or the West Indies.

Ivory boxes existed in England, but ivory was more likely to appear as inlay on containers of mahogany or highly polished ebony, while cheaper and more readily available bone inlay was employed for smaller boxes.

Interesting variations are the intricate sewing, trinket and workboxes produced by French prisoners held in English prisons during the Napoleonic Wars. Made from fragments of soup bones and odd bits of wood, these delicate and sophisticated pieces reflect the infinite time and patience lavished on them by men with little else to do. Known generally as "prisoner-of-war work," such containers are much prized by knowledgeable collectors.

Somewhat more complex were papier-mâché and straw-work boxes, both of which were generally produced in the nineteenth century by small factories. Once baked and allowed to dry, papier-mâché will take a high polish and is surprisingly sturdy. Since around 1775, English craftsmen had been using papier-mâché to make mirror cases, boxes for pens, tobacco and snuff, and handsome containers that might hold gloves or handkerchiefs, fans or sewing equipment. The sewing boxes, painted, gilded and inlaid with ivory and mother-of-pearl, are particularly attractive (plate 12).

Straw-work appears to have originated in the Near East, but since the seventeenth century it has been widely practiced on the Continent. The art may have been brought to the British Isles by French prisoners of war. Certainly the technique of inlaying designs in straw on the surface of boxes and caskets and even furniture was well established in France by the mid-seventeenth century, and the presence in England of French straw workers captured during the Napoleonic Wars greatly stimulated the English industry.

Straw-work entails splitting the straws, then glueing them onto a piece of paper in various patterns or in the form of landscapes or still lifes. These compositions are often tinted. Once completed, they are glued to boxes—generally those designed to hold jewelry and trinkets, and writing or sewing materials.

12.
Sewing box, papier-mâché, wood, mother-of-pearl, velvet, paper and ivory, painted and gilded. Surprisingly durable, papier-mâché was widely used in making boxes and even furniture during the nineteenth century. English, mid-nineteenth century. Height: 28.2 cm. (11 in.). Cooper-Hewitt Museum, bequest of Mrs. John Innes Kane

13.
Snuffbox, gold with gouache painting on paper under glass. French snuffs often bore realistic depictions of important buildings or of festivals, such as the May Day celebration depicted here. French, eighteenth century. Length: 9.5 cm. (3¾ in.). Cooper-Hewitt Museum, anonymous gift

Boxes on the Continent Every country in Europe has produced fine boxes. It is still possible to build a very substantial collection by concentrating on the products of a single nation, particularly if that country happens to be France. French craftsmen have long been fascinated with the possibilities inherent in creating small objects (known as *objets de vertu*) that are also works of art, and their boxes are among the world's finest.

The most magnificent of these creations are surely the French snuffboxes. The earliest of these containers differed little from other small receptacles of the period, the scent, patch and sweetmeats boxes. But by the beginning of the eighteenth century snuffs had begun to acquire a distinctive form of their own.

The receptacles developed into a recognizable type, one upon which the goldsmith and jeweler could lavish their finest efforts. Whether round, oval, square or oblong, or in more unusual forms—stars, shells, books, even sedan chairs—these pieces became miniature works of art. Some were mounted in gold and decorated with tiny paintings in watercolor or *gouache* (plate 13); others were sculptural creations in solid gold or silver, often set with precious jewels.

The snuffbox was transformed into a status symbol, with an importance far beyond that of a mere tobacco container. Its beauty attracted the royal eye, and such notables as Madame de Pompadour (1721–1764), who owned forty-seven examples, assembled collections. It entered into the rituals of the court and of international diplomacy, suitably engraved boxes or those bearing a likeness of the monarch being presented as signs of royal favor.

14.
Snuffbox, papier-mâché and lacquered wood with oil painting of Napoleon. Snuffs of wood and paper were inexpensive enough to be available to everyone. French, early nineteenth century. Diameter: 10 cm. (4 in.). Cooper-Hewitt Museum, bequest of Sarah Cooper Hewitt

Colorplate 7.
Oblong covered box, gold decorated with enamel and diamonds. The jeweled N is believed to stand for Napoleon, and this piece is thought to be a presentation box of the First Empire. French, early nineteenth century. Length: 8.6 cm. (3⅜ in.). Cooper-Hewitt Museum, gift of Susan Dwight Bliss

Colorplate 8.
Pill- or patch box, gold adorned with rubies and diamonds. Goldsmiths' work of this quality was the envy of Europe, and French boxes were sold throughout the Continent. French, c. 1755–56, by Julien Quévanne. Width: 5.7 cm. (2¼ in.). Cooper-Hewitt Museum, gift of Handy and Harman

The mid-eighteenth century was the high point in the production of French snuffboxes. Although they continued to be manufactured steadily during the Napoleonic era (plate 14), they gradually lost their place in the social scene. Eventually, they were relegated to the role of mere souvenirs. Yet French snuffs have always had a place in the heart of the collector. (Not too long ago, in 1979, an example in enameled gold by the craftsman Michel-Robert Hallé of Paris brought $150,000 at auction.)

The habit of giving valuable presentation boxes to favorites was also current at this time (colorplate 7), and various containers seem to have been made primarily as gifts, although their purpose remains obscure.

The French craftsmen were equally skilled in making miniature boxes to hold pills and breath sweeteners, rouge and patches (colorplate 8). Many were carved from hardstone, semiprecious minerals whose color made them exceedingly appealing. The working of hardstone took skill and patience, but the results could be quite spectacular, as in the case of a turbaned Moor complete with headdress of rubies, diamonds and turquoise set in gold and silver (colorplate 9).

French potters have long been known for the quality of their porcelain and fine earthenwares. As far back as the fourteenth century craftsmen were manufacturing *faience*, a tin-glazed earthenware featuring a white ground painted in various contrasting colors. No boxes remain from this early period, but by the mid-seventeenth

Colorplate 7

Colorplate 8

Colorplate 9

Colorplate 10

Colorplate 9.
Small box in the form of a Moor's head, carved amethyst quartz decorated with gold, silver and gems. Hardstone such as quartz was difficult to work but could render surprising results; here the natural white of the stone forms the turban. French, eighteenth century. Height: 6.4 cm. (2½ in.). Cooper-Hewitt Museum, anonymous gift

Colorplate 10.
Circular box with miniature painting on ivory, papier-mâché lacquered and embellished with mother-of-pearl, gold and tortoiseshell. Another smaller miniature, this one of a man (notably by a different artist), is concealed beneath the painting of the woman. French, c. 1768–75. Diameter: 7.9 cm. (3⅛ in.). Cooper-Hewitt Museum, anonymous gift

century small trinket and jewelry containers were being made at Rouen, Nevers and other pottery centers.

This industry gradually declined following the introduction in the 1780s of fine English creamwares. However, interesting containers from French potters who were active during the eighteenth century at towns like Strasbourg and Lyons can still be found.

Above all, the French excelled at the production of porcelain. The foundations of the great Sèvres factory were laid in 1738; a wide range of exquisite soft- and later hard-paste porcelain was to follow. Among the containers most popular with collectors are eighteenth- and nineteenth-century jewelry and powder boxes that feature one of several ground colors; *reserves* may have delicate scenes of an allegorical or pastoral nature taken from paintings by such well-known artists as Jean-Antoine Watteau (1684–1721).

Boxes from other French manufactories such as Limoges (established as a hard-paste factory in 1771) and Paris (several shops operating from about 1770) are also highly prized for their form and decoration. Later, during the nineteenth century, shops like Samson et Cie of Paris made reproductions of the English Chelsea-style porcelains complete with the fake English marks, as well as copies of such diverse wares as Sèvres and Chinese export porcelain.

French potters were active in the art pottery movement that swept Europe and the United States in the late nineteenth and early twentieth centuries. Jean Luce and the versatile Émile Gallé were among those who turned out cigarette, jewelry and powder boxes in everything from faience to porcelain and stoneware.

In contrast to their illustrious history in other mediums, French craftsmen took a long time to establish a reputation in glass. It was not until the mid-eighteenth century that such fine glassworks as those at Baccarat (1765) and Saint-Louis (1767) were established, and even then production did not include a significant quantity of boxes.

The late nineteenth century was the era of the great art glass manufacturers—Gallé; the Daum brothers, Antonin and Auguste; Amalric Walter; and René Lalique—when French glassmaking at last came into its own. Glass containers in profusion were produced in these shops, to hold powder and pins, trinkets and perfume. All are eagerly collected today. But those made in the *pâte-de-verre* technique, which involves molding a mixture of ground glass and mineral-based coloring agents, are particularly popular.

The wooden boxes and caskets of France are outstanding. Medieval caskets with domed or flat covers, bound in iron and often covered with highly elaborate floral designs or historical and mythological scenes, were used to store valuables and important papers. Smaller pieces were found in the home, while larger ones served as traveling cases. The tradition of carved decoration continued well into the

nineteenth century; even later examples in the genre retain a remarkably primitive look (plate 15). But French artisans were not restricted to the archaic style. They were capable of producing far more sophisticated wares, including lathe-turned powder and trinket boxes with complex curvilinear surface carving.

Small cardboard and paper boxes with brightly colored surfaces were used for the sale of comfits. Paper cuttings—silhouettes of people or landscapes—were often preserved under glass and used as decorative tops for the little oval or circular boxes given as tokens of appreciation. Once produced in great quantity, these fragile paper containers have disintegrated over the years, and examples in good condition are not at all common.

Closely related is papier-mâché, which in French means literally "chewed paper." The technique of working in this material was brought to France from the Near East early in the eighteenth century, and it reached a high state of development there. Among the more interesting examples are small circular boxes made of papier-mâché covered with extremely thin sheets of mother-of-pearl or tortoiseshell and embellished with oil or watercolor miniatures on ivory or paper (colorplate 10). Larger pieces in the same medium include sewing and writing boxes.

Tortoiseshell was used in combination with natural pearls to make inexpensive boxes to hold sweets or trinkets. Typically, these had bottoms and sides of paper or cardboard and shell tops, on which would be laid down an elaborate design often centering on a vase or bowl of flowers, the whole done in seed pearls pierced and strung on

15.
Covered box, carved wood with motto: VIEN MON AMI. This rather primitive container reflects a tradition of folk art carving that has long flourished in the French countryside. French, c. 1800. Length: 6.9 cm. (2 ¾ in.). Cooper-Hewitt Museum, bequest of Sarah Cooper Hewitt

16.
Covered box, paper with a glass bottom and a top of tortoiseshell, decorated with seed pearls. Due to their fragility, few of these pearl-decorated boxes have survived. French, c. 1805. Diameter: 8.5 cm. (3 ⅜ in.). Cooper-Hewitt Museum, bequest of Katherine Strong Welman

17.
Container for a pair of spectacles, shagreen on wood with silver mounts. (Glass and silver spectacles.) Tough and waterproof, shagreen was often used to protect metal objects against rust. French, eighteenth century. Length: 12.6 cm. (5 in.). Cooper-Hewitt Museum, bequest of Sarah Cooper Hewitt

16

17

fine wire (plate 16). Many hours of painstaking workmanship went into producing these tiny, fragile containers.

Again, tortoiseshell was used for the highly sophisticated technique of *boulle*. First developed by the famous French cabinetmaker André-Charles Boulle (1642–1732), the technique involved glueing together thin sheets of brass and tortoiseshell, which were then cut into complex arabesque patterns. The sheets were separated, and corresponding pieces in the two materials interchanged to create a pattern in shell and metal that was glued to a wooden frame. Boulle work took skill and time, and only a small number of boxes in the medium have survived.

Another material much used by French craftsmen was *shagreen*, which has a pebble-grained surface and is typically green in hue. Shagreen originally came from Turkey and Iran, where it was made by pressing small seeds into the untanned hides of horses, camels or wild asses. After the hides dried, the seeds were shaken out, leaving little indentations. Then the material was stained. However, by the eighteenth century lightly tanned and stained sharkskin had been found more suitable.

Shagreen, being waterproof and durable, proved particularly suitable for cases to hold metal objects that were vulnerable to rust. Eyeglasses (plate 17), knives and musical and scientific instruments could all be safely housed. But tea caddies and étuis are also to be found in this unusual material.

Caskets and jewel boxes were sometimes constructed out of ivory (plate 18); animal horn was combined with tortoiseshell (plate 19); straw-work was very popular; and by the end of the nineteenth century composition materials were coming into vogue (plate 20).

Finally, the French made all kinds of metal boxes. The most desirable of these are in solid gold or silver, often embossed or engraved or both, in some instances inlaid or even encrusted with precious and semiprecious stones. Aside from snuffs, other forms range from the smallest pill, comfit and perfume containers (plate 21) to large boxes to hold documents and jewelry, and traveling boxes.

Less valuable but often no less interesting are receptacles of iron, tin, brass and copper. The early French iron boxes resemble those of the same period made in wood and were frequently fitted with elaborate locks to preserve the contents. Brass and copper tobacco boxes were usually turned ("spun") to shape on a lathe, and might have highly detailed incised or engraved surface decoration. Both tin and toleware containers were intended primarily for sale to the working and farm classes. These pieces featured a bright peasant-style decoration set against a black, red, yellow or green ground.

The potters in what is now Germany are renowned for their high-quality stoneware and for the porcelain produced at Meissen, near

18.
Casket of carved ivory with gold mounts. Allegorical decoration such as this was very popular during the eighteenth and early nineteenth centuries. French, eighteenth century. Length: 7.5 cm. (3 in.). Musée des Arts Décoratifs, Paris

19.
Snuffbox, animal horn and tortoiseshell, inscribed BOITE ROYALE DE FRANCE ANNEE 1823. French, 1823. Diameter: 9.8 cm. (3⅞ in.). Cooper-Hewitt Museum, gift of Mrs. James A. Roosevelt

20.
Covered box with intaglio decoration, cast-composition material. French, early twentieth century; designed by René Lalique (1860–1945), the well-known glassmaker. Width: 7.8 cm. (3⅛ in.). Metropolitan Museum of Art, New York, gift of Edward C. Moore, Jr., 1924

18

19

20

21

22

21.
Scent box, silver with pierced decoration. The French made large numbers of silver containers both for use at home and for sale abroad. French, c. 1750–52. Height: 8.5 cm. (3⅜ in.). Musée des Arts Décoratifs, Paris

22.
Oval, hinged box, enamel on base metal with copper-gilt mounts and hand-painted scenes. Probably made in Dresden, this piece is characteristic of high-quality German enamelwares. German, late eighteenth century. Length: 8.9 cm. (3½ in.). Cooper-Hewitt Museum, gift of Katherine Strong Welman

23.
Bride's box, wood steamed and bent together, then paint-decorated. These colorful folk boxes were traditionally given to the new bride. German, 1797. Length: 48.1 cm. (19 in.). Cooper-Hewitt Museum, gift of Hamill and Barker

23

24.
Patch box, wood lacquered black. Top covered with hand-tinted engraving, triple face of Christ. The use of an engraving rather than an original painting reflects the approach of mass-production methods. German, late eighteenth century. Diameter: 9.3 cm. (3⅝ in.). Cooper-Hewitt Museum, gift of the estate of Mrs. Lathrop Colgate

Dresden, and other prominent centers. Indeed, the first European porcelain was made at Meissen, and since 1710 the factory there has turned out all kinds of objects, including dresser and storage boxes decorated with the elaborate painted landscapes for which it is so well known. Enamelware is also highly prized, and the best examples (plate 22) compare favorably with French products.

Equally typical in another genre are the wooden peasant-made bride's boxes (also known as chip boxes) produced in rural areas from medieval times until the turn of this century. The custom of donating a small decorated box or casket as a wedding gift goes back a long way; German-made examples were already so highly thought of in the fifteenth century that they were being exported to surrounding countries.

Bride's boxes, which are quite large, are generally oval or round in form. They are made by steaming or soaking thin strips of birch or maple until soft, then bending the strips around a thicker base and securing them with wooden pegs or iron nails. Some boxes are decorated with incised patterns, but most have elaborate painted designs. Initially, these consisted of nothing more than swirling patterns on a contrasting *marbleized* background, but by the eighteenth century the pieces were being decorated with stylized portraits of men and women in period costumes (plate 23). In the nineteenth century the originality and artistic quality of these containers gradually declined. The examples made today for tourist sale bear little resemblance to their predecessors, but the earlier boxes are extremely popular with collectors, who sometimes mistake them for very similar pieces made in the United States by Germanic immigrants.

Smaller, more delicate boxes were also made in Germany. Some were covered with shallow incised decoration or with *chip carving*;

others, primarily factory-made examples, might be ornamented with a watercolor or engraving (plate 24), which was glued to the top of the round or oval box, then either varnished or covered with a thin sheet of glass. Most such containers were less than ten inches in diameter, designed to hold sweets or small personal items. Many were sold as souvenirs of pilgrimages to religious shrines or historical sites.

Some of the very earliest boxes of the area represented a combination of wood with iron. Typically, an iron framework or an iron top would be combined with panels of linden or walnut. Examples dated to the thirteenth century have been preserved, sometimes covered with stylized animal and vegetable motifs in tempera on a *gesso* base (plate 25). Needless to say, pieces of this vintage are neither plentiful nor inexpensive.

Boxes were constructed of iron alone, many of them again dating from the late medieval period. Incised or painted decoration was common, as were the complex and visually appealing locking devices typical of the same era. Being intended for storage or traveling, these boxes were generally large, but three- or four-inch jewel caskets existed. Smaller containers in silver were also made; some, such as the snuffs (plate 26) and pillboxes, were enameled in the French manner.

The German copper mines at Mansfield are Europe's oldest. Craftsmen have been working the metal there for over seven hundred years, turning out a range of copper vessels, including tinder- and spice boxes. More common examples in brass include engraved tobacco containers and wheel-turned snuffs and pillboxes. As the Continent's leading producer of pewter, Germany is particularly noted for its elegant pewter boxes to hold sugar, spices and condiments.

25.
Casket or box, lindenwood bound in iron and decorated with tempera on a gesso base. Medieval painted wooden containers are rare in Germany and elsewhere. German, upper Rhine region, late thirteenth century. Length: 26.5 cm. (10⅜ in.). Metropolitan Museum of Art, New York, gift of J. Pierpont Morgan, by exchange, 1976

26

26.
Snuffbox, silver with a cover of enamel on copper. This piece was decorated by C. F. Heroldt (1700–1779), one of many painters who earned their livelihood as enamel decorators. German, c. 1730–50. Length: 7.6 cm. (3 in.). Cooper-Hewitt Museum, bequest of Sarah Cooper Hewitt

27.
Casket, wood covered with pastiglia (molded and carved gesso) and parcel gilt. This piece is in the early Renaissance style, although the figural decoration is almost medieval. Northern Italian, c. 1500. Length: 16 cm. (6¼ in.). Cooper-Hewitt Museum, purchase of Friends of the Museum Fund

27

28

28.
Casket, oak covered with tooled leather; silk lining and an iron lock. During the Renaissance period leather tooling was a widely practiced art. Italian, sixteenth century. Length: 25 cm. (9⅞ in.). Cooper-Hewitt Museum, gift of Mrs. Max Farrand

29.
Reliquary box, carved and pierced bone with gold foil. The extraordinary detail and sophisticated composition of this container reflect the great skills of the late medieval craftsmen. Northern Italian, tenth century. Height: 18.6 cm. (7¼ in.). Metropolitan Museum of Art, New York, Cloisters Collection, 1953

29

In Italy during the period of the Renaissance (c. 1400–1550), craftsmen made chests, coffers and boxes in a plethora of materials, and this tradition of versatility and experimentation continued through succeeding centuries. In one method, *pastiglia*—a claylike composition with a gesso base—was applied to a wooden core and molded by hand to create remarkable raised decoration (plate 27). In another, leather was first softened by soaking in water, then stretched over wood and finally tooled to create unusual surface effects (plate 28). Although it is less commonly used today, leather is very suitable for containers. When wet, it stretches and can be shaped and worked almost like clay. It takes paint easily, and can also be decorated by piercing or by adding brass tacks or studs. Boxes and small trunks made of wood covered with leather were common throughout Europe for hundreds of years.

The Italians were adept at working in ivory and bone, both of which were used for containers. Sizable coffers or *reliquary* boxes have been found in the abbeys of northern Italy. The extraordinary detail of the pierced and shaped decoration of these late medieval pieces rivals the finest bone and ivory carving of the Far East (plate 29).

Mosaic work in stone and glass was also characteristic of Italy. Some of the loveliest of these pieces are the delicate little boxes for snuff, trinkets and comfits. Decorated with highly realistic renditions of buildings and interiors, these mosaic compositions are made up of hundreds of tiny pieces of marble, agate and other stones carefully fitted together within a round or oval metal framework (plate 30). In some cases the mosaics occupy the entire surface of a box top; in others they fit within a reserve against a background of agate, porphyry or another colorful stone (plate 31). First made during the eighteenth century, these pieces became very popular in the century that followed.

Horn and other natural materials were used. Snuffboxes, as popular in Italy as everywhere on the Continent, were often made out of horn. A typical combination was a pressed horn container and cover banded in gold with pierced decoration (plate 32). Shagreen was also employed, primarily in the manufacture of tea caddies (plate 33).

And, of course, gold, silver and precious stones went into the creation of small boxes that were in their own way works of art. Some of the finest of these creations emerged from the sixteenth century, but even a hundred years ago Italian goldsmiths were producing luxury containers for a highly sophisticated clientele.

During the eighteenth and nineteenth centuries craftsmen in Austria manufactured snuff-, patch and pillboxes out of gold, silver and other metals that were quite similar to those produced in surrounding areas.

30.
Round box, marble mosaic with variegated agate and gold mounts. The Roman hall pictured on this piece is made up of hundreds of tiny fragments of colored marble. Italian, probably Rome, nineteenth century. Diameter: 7.3 cm. (2⅞ in.). Cooper-Hewitt Museum, anonymous gift

31.
Snuffbox, green porphyry decorated with marble mosaic and mounted in gold. The classical decoration is typical of such mosaic boxes. Italian, c. 1840. Length: 7.5 cm. (3 in.). Cooper Hewitt Museum, bequest of Sarah Cooper Hewitt

32.
Snuffbox, body of gold with a horn lid overlaid with pierced-gold decoration representing the tale of Leda and the Swan. Although not as popular as in France, snuffboxes were used and appreciated in Italy. Italian, early eighteenth century. Diameter: 6.5 cm. (2½ in.). Cooper-Hewitt Museum, bequest of Sarah Cooper Hewitt

33.
Tea caddy, shagreen over a wooden core with silver mounts. The interior of this hexagonal tea caddy is of polished walnut. Italian, early nineteenth century. Height: 16.5 cm. (6½ in.). Cooper-Hewitt Museum, gift of Mrs. James O. Green

30

32

31

33

34.
Circular box, brass tooled and engraved. The seal within this box is that of Leopold II (1747–1792) of the House of Hapsburg-Lorraine. Austrian, c. 1790–92. Diameter: 8.6 cm. (3⅜ in.). Cooper-Hewitt Museum, gift of the estate of Mrs. Lathrop Colgate Harper

As befitted the seat of the Holy Roman Empire, *seal boxes* in brass bore the mark of the House of Hapsburg (plate 34).

At the turn of the century, Vienna was the center of the artistic ferment that led to the development of modern industrial design. Among the guiding lights of this movement was Josef Hoffmann (1870–1956), director of the famed Wiener Werkstätte (Vienna Workshops) and himself a designer of boxes (plate 35).

Peasant artisans in rural Austria turned out a variety of handcrafted wooden containers, some carved from solid blocks of wood, others formed in the same manner as the German bride's boxes, which they closely resembled in shape and decoration.

Equally appealing folk art boxes were made in the mountain hamlets of Switzerland. A typical form is the storage box in the shape of a peasant's hut (plate 36). With its top shaped like a sloping roof, and the body completely covered with bright floral forms, including indigenous flowers and shrubs, such a piece is the quintessence of folk art.

But the Swiss could also produce the most sophisticated containers. Their snuffboxes in enameled gold, silver gilt or tortoiseshell compare favorably with similar French pieces. And no other nation has rivaled the remarkable range of music boxes, ranging in form from tiny musical snuffs to large sewing and workboxes, credited to this small country.

Dutch artisans liked to work with natural materials. Their snuffs, often octagonal, were made with carefully etched or incised pictorial scenes cut into a piece of mother-of-pearl. Urban and rural scenes and views of the great sailing ships that made Holland a world power in the seventeenth century (plate 37) are common. Similar decoration

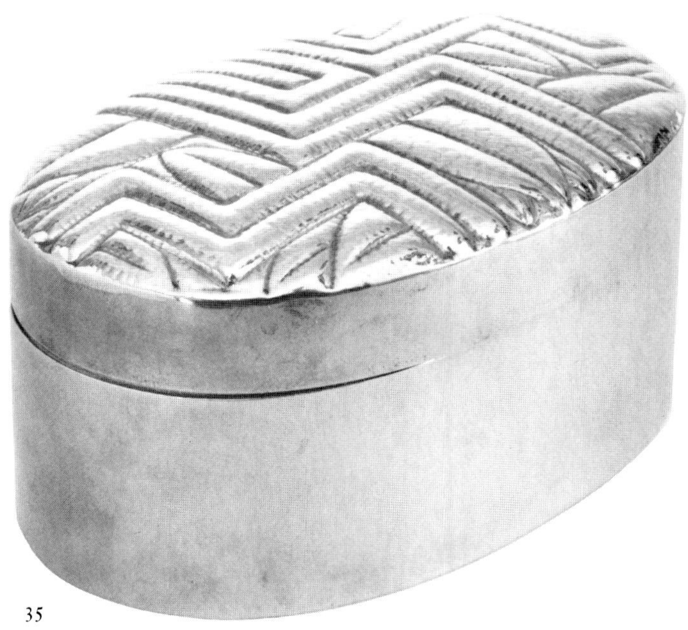
35

35.
Oval box, machined and embossed brass, designed by Josef Hoffmann, director of the Wiener Werkstätte during the 1920s. Austrian, c. 1920. Length: 17.3 cm. (6¾ in.). Cooper-Hewitt Museum, gift of Mrs. Phelps Warren

36.
Storage box, polychrome painted wood in the form of an Alpine peasant's hut. The bright floral decoration on this piece is typical of rural folk art throughout central Europe. Swiss, seventeenth century. Length: 27.9 cm. (11 in.). Metropolitan Museum of Art, New York, Rogers Fund, 1908

37.
Octagonal snuffbox, silver with top of etching-decorated mother-of-pearl. During the seventeenth century Holland was a major sea power, and Dutch accessories were often embellished with representations of ships. Dutch, seventeenth century. Length: 11.1 cm. (4⅜ in.). Cooper-Hewitt Museum, gift of Sarah Cooper Hewitt

36

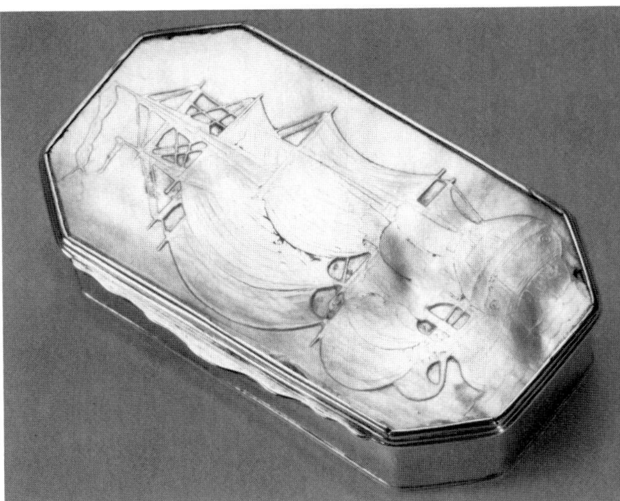
37

38

appeared on the brass repoussé tobacco boxes for which Dutch craftsmen are justly famous.

Other containers from The Netherlands were manufactured out of tortoiseshell, papier-mâché and shagreen (plate 38). The nécessaires are particularly striking. Usually less than four by eight inches, these containers can hold a surprising number of little objects—thimbles, scissors, rules, powder boxes and even mirrors.

Containers from Scandinavia are comparatively less plentiful. Surrounded by great stretches of forest, these northern craftsmen turned first to wood, so that from the fifteenth century most Swedish, Norwegian and Finnish boxes were wooden ones. The Swedes were especially adept at carving containers in the form of animals (plate 39). Often these pieces would be completely covered with close-set chipwork decoration, primarily in geometric and floral motifs, although realistic renditions of animals, men and legendary beasts were popular.

Norwegian boxes resembled those of Germany and central Europe in construction. Made of birch soaked or steamed to give it flexibility, then wrapped around a pine or fir base and secured with fiber or leather thongs, such containers were usually decorated by *incising*, by

38.
Nécessaire, shagreen on a wooden core with silver mounts and applied decoration. The nécessaire was used by ladies to hold such small objects as scissors, tweezers, needles and pencils. Dutch, nineteenth century. Height: 10 cm. (3⅞ in.). Cooper-Hewitt Museum, gift of Mrs. James Roosevelt, in loving memory of Mrs. James O. Green

39.
Swing-top wooden box carved in the form of a duck with geometric chip-carved decoration. Chip or gouge carving is an old form of decoration that has remained popular throughout most of Europe. Swedish, dated 1759. Height: 28 cm. (11 in.). Smithsonian Institution, National Museum of American History

39

40.
Telescoping wooden box, of wood steamed and lapped, then sewn together; decorated with paint-filled incised motifs. Boxes made from strips of wood are found in Europe and parts of North America. Probably Norwegian, nineteenth century. Height: 14 cm. (5½ in.). Smithsonian Institution, National Museum of American History

painting or by a combination of both methods (plate 40). Painting was especially popular in Norway, where the technique of *rosemaling* (rose painting) was developed in the mid-eighteenth century. Based on the appearance of rococo ornamentation, this involved covering an entire surface with stylized flower and leaf motifs executed in bold hues: red, green, yellow and blue. Although it was seldom practiced in other Scandinavian countries, rosemaling remained popular in Norway until the late nineteenth century and spread from there to the midwestern United States.

Northern craftsmen also created more sophisticated work. During the eighteenth century Danish goldsmiths put out snuffs and other small boxes in enamel on gold that were comparable to similar pieces being produced elsewhere in Europe (plate 41). Such miniature containers in gold and silver (plate 42) were made throughout this region.

Since 1900, and particularly after World War II, Scandinavia has become an important ceramic center. Finely made tea caddies (plate 43), powder boxes and jewelry containers in the modern style have come from such major commercial potteries as Bing & Grøndahl and Royal Copenhagen in Denmark, as well as from Sweden.

41

41.
Covered box, gold enameled and mounted with a miniature oil portrait. Although not widely distributed, Danish boxes in precious metals are of high quality. Danish, late eighteenth century. Diameter: 7.9 cm. (3⅛ in.). Metropolitan Museum of Art, New York, gift of J. Pierpont Morgan, 1917

42

42.
Small covered box, repoussé silver. Miniature containers like this served to hold everything from pills to postage stamps. Norwegian, 1848. Length: 4.6 cm. (1¾ in.). Cooper-Hewitt Museum, gift of Eleanor Garnier Hewitt

43

43.
Tea caddy, celadon-glaze earthenware. Although late in developing, the Scandinavian ceramics industry has been in the forefront of modern design. Swedish, c. 1925. Height: 15.3 cm. (6⅛ in.). Cooper-Hewitt Museum, gift of Mr. H. Wade White

In Russia, under the czars, craftsmen were expected to maintain very high standards, and the court commissioned superb containers. Most famous of all are the jewel-encrusted pieces, many in the form of Easter eggs, that were produced for the royal court by the designer Peter Carl Fabergé (1846–1920), who was of Huguenot extraction. These extraordinary pieces, set in gold, silver and platinum, were very precisely made and might even conceal the workings of elaborate music boxes. Smaller, slightly less costly eggs and cigarette cases, among other items, continued to be made by the Fabergé factory for members of Russian and European society. Today, a Fabergé egg (colorplate 11) is an expensive rarity.

Of an equally high standard were the small containers produced by the silversmiths of Moscow to hold snuff, pills, comfits and tobacco. These were often gilt-lined and decorated in *niello*—a form of inlay work in which tiny designs were incised into the surface of a silver object, then filled with a black amalgam to provide dramatic contrast

Colorplate 11.
Casket, Renaissance style, agate mounted in gold and enameled; set with diamonds and rubies. Designed by Peter Carl Fabergé (1846–1920), this egg-shaped container was a gift to Czar Alexander III. Russian, dated 1894. Height: 13.3 cm. (5¼ in.). Forbes Magazine Collection, New York

44.
Snuffbox, gold decorated with enamel. Many Russian boxes were very elaborate, but simple, elegant examples were also produced. Russian, late eighteenth century. Length: 8.9 cm. (3½ in.). Cooper-Hewitt Museum, gift of Susan Dwight Bliss

Colorplate 12.
Lift-top box, silver with niello-work inlay and a gilt lining. Niello is an amalgam of powdered silver, lead, copper, sulphur, and sometimes borax, which is used to emphasize incised decoration in silver. Russian, Moscow, c. 1780. Length: 8.2 cm. (3¼ in.). Metropolitan Museum of Art, New York, bequest of John L. Cadwalader, 1914

(colorplate 12). The niello technique (developed at the time of the Roman Empire) reached its zenith in Russia during the late nineteenth century. Other luxury boxes were enameled (plate 44), or both enameled and set with precious stones (plate 45).

From the sixteenth century, carvers in the White Sea ports of Archangel and Kholmogory were producing high-quality containers of wood sheathed in carved and engraved walrus ivory. Sewing boxes, coffers and elaborate dressing table sets that included lift-top containers in all kinds of shapes (round, oval, square, oblong and heart) were made. This craft proved so popular with the nobility that in 1649 Czar Alexis I Mikhailovich (reigned 1645–76) declared it a state monopoly. Today, early Russian ivory carving is relatively uncommon and correspondingly expensive. The Russians have also produced interesting and sophisticated lacquer boxes.

45.
Scrolled lift-top box, gold enameled and set with precious jewels. This is a presentation box bearing the cipher of Czar Nicholas II (1868–1918). Russian, c. 1896–1903. Length: 9.8 cm. (3⅞ in.). Metropolitan Museum of Art, New York, gift of J. Pierpont Morgan, 1917

46.
Octagonal covered box, wood inlaid with bone and other woods in contrasting hues. The Hispano-Moresque style of this box arose out of the confluence of Islamic and Spanish cultures. Spanish, fifteenth to sixteenth century. Height: 14.9 cm. (5⅞ in.). Metropolitan Museum of Art, New York, Rogers Fund, 1950

On a simpler level, peasant craftsmen have long produced variants on brightly decorated boxes. Here we should include the well-known sets of stacking dolls, in which smaller figures are concealed within ever larger ones. This appealing folk art is quite similar to that practiced elsewhere in Eastern Europe, in Poland, Hungary and Yugoslavia, for example. Country-made containers from this region are still crafted for use at home and for sale to tourists.

Folk arts flourish in the Iberian Peninsula, where rural artisans in both Spain and Portugal continue to produce interesting containers. Portuguese products include boxes made of cork lightly carved and painted with typical village scenes, often the local *corrida* (bullfight). From Spain come pipe and tobacco boxes in both hard and soft woods, some painted, some simply notch-carved in elaborate geometric patterns, and some elaborately inlaid with bone (plate 46).

But the Spanish craftsmen are known above all for their ironwork. Iron was being mined in Spain as early as the sixth century B.C., and by the Middle Ages swords of Spanish steel were highly prized. The Spanish boxes are typically rectangular, with domed or flat tops. They are of wrought rather than cast iron, and are often formed over a wooden core with complex decorative motifs engraved or laid down in fine iron wire (plate 47). Most are large and generally have ornate, rather complicated-looking locks.

In closing, it should be stressed that this brief discussion of European boxes cannot possibly do justice to the diversity available. Exciting opportunities await the patient collector.

47.
Casket or coffer, wrought iron with engraved decoration. The Spanish have long been renowned for their iron work, and wrought storage or jewelry boxes were among their finest creations. Spanish, sixteenth century. Length: 13 cm. (5⅛ in.). Cooper-Hewitt Museum, gift of Susan Dwight Bliss

4 Near Eastern and African Boxes

Containers found among the peoples who inhabit those lands bordering the eastern and southern Mediterranean differ substantially in materials and in style from those made in central and southern Africa. But both categories afford desirable additions to any collection.

The Near East The artisans of the Near East were influenced in varying degrees—depending upon their location and particular cultural circumstances—by artistic impulses emanating from Europe and from Asia. In the northeast, around Constantinople, last stronghold of the Roman Empire, Greek and Roman styles often prevailed long after the area had been overrun by Islamic forces. Some small caskets or boxes were decorated with human figures in classical garb and pose that bore a distinct relationship to examples found farther west (colorplate 14). Islamic ivories from the same period were decorated in quite a different manner, reflecting a much more abstract approach (plate 48).

People in Byzantium, as it was known, had cultivated a taste for opulence; the perfume boxes and containers for toiletries from this area were frequently made of gold, silver, jade or finely carved ivory. Many were studded with gems or bound with gold and silver bands. The church reliquaries were equally sumptuous.

The Islamic peoples to the south and east were just as fond of show, but their containers are generally of more modest materials, worked with great care and skill. Some of the world's finest ceramics come from the area that is present-day Syria, Iran and Turkey. By about the ninth century ceramicists in these areas had developed the art of glazing a red clay body with an opaque white tin glaze upon which designs might be painted in contrasting colors. Tin-glazed

Colorplate 13.
Casket, brass engraved and inlaid with silver. The art of inlaying silver in another less precious metal, termed damascene work, has long been practiced in the Near East. This box was probably used as a container for jewelry, gems or other small, precious objects. Syrian, fifteenth century. Length: 17 cm. (6⅝ in.). Metropolitan Museum of Art, New York, bequest of Edward C. Moore, 1891

48.
Ivory lift-top box, bound in gold and studded with semiprecious stones. Religious strictures prevented Islamic artists from portraying the human figure, and their decorative motifs are, in general, more abstract than those from cultures farther west. Siculo-Arabic, twelfth century. Length: 17.1 cm. (6¾ in.). Metropolitan Museum of Art, New York, gift of Mr. Alastair Bradley Martin, 1972

Colorplate 14.
Domed lift-top casket, carved ivory with gold fixtures. The form and decoration of boxes made in and about Constantinople reflected the influence of the ancient Roman Empire. Byzantium, A.D. 1150–1200. Length: 28.9 cm. (11⅜ in.). Metropolitan Museum of Art, New York, gift of J. Pierpont Morgan, 1917

wares were long one of the world's most important forms of pottery. Containers in this medium include those designed to hold medicines and unusual six- and eight-sided storage boxes.

The earliest of these pieces show Chinese influence, with local versions of the classical scenes of mountains and court processions so much favored by the potters of China. Once Islam was established in the seventh century, however, such scenes were modified to satisfy the tenets of a faith that opposed any representations of the human figure and encouraged the use of geometric and abstract design. As a result, Near Eastern boxes came to be decorated with scrolls, arabesques and a great deal of calligraphy spelling out divine blessings or simply the names of the owners of these pieces.

Later, when active trade developed between the Near East and the West, Syrian and Iranian potters began to use a more realistic style, particularly for export items. Westernized houses, ships and even human figures appeared. For home consumption, though, geometric designs often based on textile and abstracted floral patterns continued to be preferred.

The Near Eastern craftsmen were equally skilled with other materials. Bronze was being worked as far back as the third millennium B.C., and artisans in the area produced boxes in the shapes of various animals at that time. During the reign of the Seljuks (1071–1157), cast decoration was enhanced by the addition of engraving and by the use of inlay in silver and gold.

49

50

49.
Pen case (kalamdan), painted and lacquered papier-mâché. Although not as widely practiced as it was in the Orient, the art of lacquering was well known among the Near Eastern peoples. Iranian, eighteenth century. Length: 23.5 cm. (9¼ in.). Metropolitan Museum of Art, New York, bequest of Mrs. Amery R. Sheldon, 1908

50.
Writing box, red leather with stamped, gilded and painted decoration. Islamic leatherwork had a significant influence on the craft as practiced farther west, most notably in the Iberian Peninsula, where it became an important decorative art. Turkish, c. 1600. Length: 37.5 cm. (14¾ in.). Metropolitan Museum of Art, New York, Rogers Fund, 1933

Thirteenth-century Syrian craftsmen were employing inlay to decorate brass and copper as well as bronze, and the technique of *damascene* work (the skill originated in the city of Damascus) was highly developed. The method involves inlaying a precious metal—silver or gold—into a less precious metal such as brass, copper or iron. In this way, very complex designs can be created (colorplate 13).

Cloisonné work was also practiced at an early date in the area. The technique of cloisonné involves soldering thin strips of metal to the surface of a bronze (or copper) vessel. These tiny metal walls form cloisons into which liquid enamels are poured. Once fired and polished, the contrasting colors can take on a jewel-like quality. Islamic shops today still produce good examples of cloisonné as well as of enamel painting on brass. Brass was used by the Syrians to make finely engraved writing boxes that were covered with arabesque designs and geometric figures. Copper boxes were decorated with inlay or enameled, particularly by the Turks; and iron treasure or money boxes with complex locks were made throughout the region.

Natural materials came into play. The Iranians in particular were very skilled at creating wooden and papier-mâché storage, toilet and writing boxes, which they either painted in traditional designs or lacquered (plate 49). Elaborate jewel boxes in ivory would often be covered with incised arabesques or animal figures and bound in brass or gold, studded with precious or semiprecious stones. Other materials that are found less often include leather and certain minerals. The leather might be soaked, then woven or shaped into box form (plates 50 and 51). Minerals such as alabaster and quartz could be carved into small containers.

Glass was known in the Near East long before the time of Christ; indeed, much of the so-called Roman glass was actually manufactured in this area. The Syrians developed the technique of enameling glass in the thirteenth century. Since that time numerous fine examples in this medium, including boxes, have been produced in such major centers as Aleppo and Damascus. A good deal of the skill that rendered the Venetian glassmakers justly famous was acquired through contacts with the Near East.

Today, boxmaking in the traditional style continues. Craftsmen still create brass boxes for sale to tourists, often using metal hammered out from the shell cases left after the many wars that have plagued the area. Although these twentieth-century containers from Lebanon, Turkey, Syria and Iran usually lack the artistic quality of the earlier work, they are relatively plentiful and offer an interesting field for the collector.

51.
Box in the shape of a heart, crimson-colored leather, stamped and gilded. Arabesque designs are a common decorative motif in Near Eastern art. Iranian, eighteenth century. Width: 12.7 cm. (5 in.). Metropolitan Museum of Art, New York, bequest of Edward C. Moore, 1891

Africa The people living along the southern coast of the Mediterranean were strongly influenced by the arts and crafts of Syria and Iran. Not surprisingly, the boxes from that area, which are primarily of metal and pottery, closely resemble those made farther east.

The Nubians, neighbors and often bitter rivals of the Egyptians from the sixth to the fourteenth century, produced some early containers that were highly sophisticated in style and technique. Jewel caskets, storage and cosmetic boxes of wood sheathed in bronze and inlaid in ivory (colorplate 15) have all been found at sites associated with the culture.

To the south, a very different culture predominated. Crafts centered on the various tribal dynasties that once controlled Africa. The African artisans lived for the most part in areas isolated from prolonged contact with either Eastern or Western influences. Until the early nineteenth century they developed their own unique form and style for every kind of craft, including those techniques utilized in creating boxes to store food, clothing, religious objects and precious metals such as gold dust.

Customs and actual practice varied from one tribe to another, but boxmaking was an ancient and venerated tradition. The craftsmen's methods and designs had been developed over centuries. Wood was the traditional medium: it was present in abundance and easily worked with the rather crude tools available to the local artists, most of whom owned nothing more than a rasp and a double-bladed knife.

Once again, form and decoration were frequently related to the styles of other mediums. A wooden box might resemble one made concurrently or more often at an earlier period out of bone or stone; the surface design resulting from the construction of a basket or a rug might be copied in the woven pattern carved into a wooden surface (plate 52). African boxmaking is closely related to other crafts carried on within a specific tribe, and knowledgeable collectors can often recognize the origin of a container, even though there is rarely a signature.

Colorplate 15.
Box with slide top, wood inlaid with ivory and bound in bronze. The Nubians, who were neighbors of the Egyptians, created interesting and attractive boxes; unfortunately, only a few examples have survived. Nubian, North Africa, third century A.D. Height: 16.5 cm. (6½ in.). University Museum, University of Pennsylvania

The decorative carving on African boxes must always be thought of in the context of effigy carving—the most important aspect of the continent's art. Carvers devoted much of their time to making statues, masks and other ritual objects associated with religious worship, ancestor cults, and the various men's and women's societies that dominated the social life of almost every tribe.

These effigies were not primarily realistically carved, in that a figure was shaped to reveal its "spirit" rather than its actual appearance; in most cases, the beings portrayed were gods or supernatural creatures. This tendency to abstraction was carried over to every aspect of wood carving. African boxes are typically adorned with highly abstract anthropomorphic forms or with geometric devices—

52

52.
Paint box, carved wood. Most African boxes were made of wood, and many were related in form and decoration to earlier containers of bone or basketry materials. African, former Belgian Congo, Bakuba tribe, nineteenth century. Length: 20 cm. (8 in.). Brooklyn Museum, New York, Museum Expedition, 1922

53.
Mortar box with swing lid and handle, carved wood. Highly abstract incised decoration was common on many African boxes of the late nineteenth and early twentieth centuries. African, Zaire, nineteenth century. Length: 26 cm. (10¼ in.). Brooklyn Museum, New York, Museum Expedition, 1922

triangles, squares, circles, diagonals—all of which had symbolic meaning (plate 53).

Boxes also took the form of actual objects. A storage container might resemble a gabled house of the very sort occupied by its maker (plate 54) or the shape of an animal or human figure (colorplate 16). As early as the thirteenth century, the cities of Ife and later Benin in what is now Nigeria produced remarkable cast-bronze sculptures in the form of humans, gods and animals. These unusual examples are believed to reflect knowledge of the bronze caster's art passed on by Arab traders. In any case, one of the most common and appealing of the bronzes is in the shape of a leopard's head. Sometime in the late nineteenth or early twentieth century a wood carver in Benin reproduced this same leopard's head as a wooden box (plate 55), creating an accurate rendition of the original, right down to the bronze studs seen on fifteenth-century Benin examples.

Bronze boxes are quite uncommon in Africa, although the Ashanti people of Ghana make gold and brass boxes. Both are closely allied to their religion and their culture. The Ashanti believe gold to be a symbol of life and power; it is also the royal color. Over the past several hundred years a variety of gold objects have appeared, among the most important of which are the golden containers known

53

54

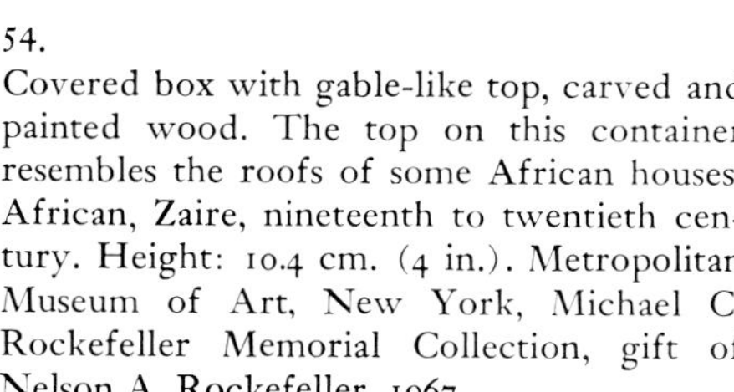

54.
Covered box with gable-like top, carved and painted wood. The top on this container resembles the roofs of some African houses. African, Zaire, nineteenth to twentieth century. Height: 10.4 cm. (4 in.). Metropolitan Museum of Art, New York, Michael C. Rockefeller Memorial Collection, gift of Nelson A. Rockefeller, 1967

55.
Box in the form of a feline head, carved wood. This piece was clearly patterned after a much earlier Benin cast-bronze leopard's head. African, Nigeria, late nineteenth to early twentieth century. Length: 17.2 cm. (6¾ in.). Brooklyn Museum, New York, gift of A. and P. Peralta-Ramos

Colorplate 16.
Tobacco container in the form of a seated chieftain, carved wood. Boxes in the shapes of deities or humans often had ritual purposes. African, Angola, late nineteenth to early twentieth century. Height: 22.8 cm. (9 in.). Brooklyn Museum, New York, gift of Mr. and Mrs. John A. Friede

55

56.
Box for the storage of gold dust, cast brass with incised and applied decoration. Gold had religious and political significance to the Ashanti of Ghana, and great effort and skill were devoted to making the containers in which the precious dust was stored. African, Ghana, nineteenth to twentieth century. Length: 9.6 cm. (3¾ in.). Metropolitan Museum of Art, New York, Michael C. Rockefeller Memorial Collection, bequest of Nelson A. Rockefeller, 1969

57.
Rectangular covered box with basketwork decoration, carved ivory. Although ivory was often used in Africa for masks and smaller objects, boxes in this material are surprisingly uncommon. African, Congo, Kuba tribe, late nineteenth to early twentieth century. Length: 20.3 cm. (8 in.). Brooklyn Museum, New York, gift of Mr. John Hewitt

as Kudos, intended to house the souls of tribal ancestors. So significant is the precious metal to this people that it can be worked only by royal craftsmen who are hereditary practitioners of the goldsmiths' craft, passing down their skills and tools to their sons.

The Ashanti also worked brass, which was made into weights for measuring gold, and they produced small but often very elaborate brass boxes in which to store the precious gold dust (plate 56). Gold-dust boxes are still being cast in Ghana and are relatively plentiful. Like the weights, they are popularly collected as a form of miniature sculpture unique to Africa.

Sometimes seen are small boxes carved from elephant ivory, long plentiful in certain parts of Africa. The abstract, geometric designs, like those on wooden boxes, are clearly related to basketry and textile weaves (plate 57). Other African boxmaking materials include leather, gourds and animal bone. The last was used primarily for smaller examples to hold snuff and powder once these substances had been introduced by Europeans. Like so much African woodenware, the carving on such pieces is of a very high order.

African boxes are now extremely popular, and they are available in large quantities. Would-be purchasers should, however, be aware that the great majority of such objects on the market today, particularly the wooden ones, are of very recent manufacture. The difference in value between a nineteenth-century carved and painted African box and one made just a few years ago is considerable, but it often takes a knowledgeable individual to distinguish between the two.

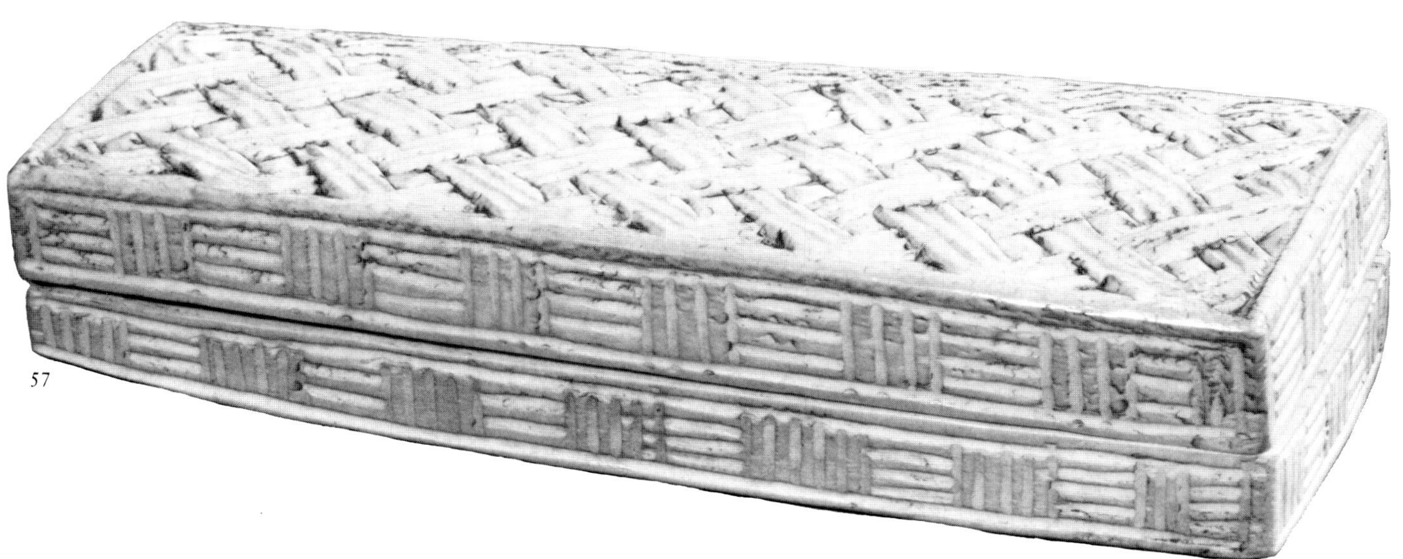

57

5 Boxes of Asia and the Pacific

A preponderance of the oldest and most fascinating boxes come from the Orient, reflecting its extraordinary diversity of cultures. The highly sophisticated metal, ivory and lacquer boxes of China and Japan stand in stark contrast to the naive pieces produced in Polynesia and certain parts of Southeast Asia.

China As in discussing so many other Asian antiquities, a survey of Oriental boxes should start with China, where some of the first known boxes were produced nearly two thousand years ago. Not surprisingly, surviving examples are of metal, specifically bronze—a material the Chinese are said to have discovered in the third millennium B.C. Exotic-looking bronze boxes with peaked, rooflike tops (colorplate 17) have been found in the tombs of the Shang dynasty (1766–1122 B.C.). Archaeologists believe that these boxes served as ritual funeral vessels or as food, drink and cosmetic containers.

The early Chinese bronzes were cast from a metal containing approximately 88 parts copper to 12 parts tin, a hard and durable medium, well calculated to survive the passage of time. The surfaces of such pieces are decorated with complex linear forms featuring geometric and abstracted animal motifs as well as those found on basketwork. Many bear lengthy statements in Chinese script: imperial edicts, commendations to the recipient, even land grants.

The Chinese have continued to make bronze boxes. During the nineteenth and early twentieth centuries large numbers were produced for sale to European markets. These include superb snuff- and sewing boxes, some covered with engraved decoration, others enameled in cloisonné.

The early bronze boxes were very expensive; indeed, an ancient definition of the wealthy was "those who eat from bronze vessels to

Colorplate 17.
Covered ritual vessel, cast bronze. Elaborately decorated containers such as this have been found in many early Chinese tombs. They were used as funeral offerings. Chinese, Shang dynasty, fifteenth to twelfth century B.C. Height: 25.4 cm. (10 in.). Metropolitan Museum of Art, New York, anonymous gift, 1974

the music of bronze bells." Silver by contrast was used sparingly in China, as generally throughout Asia, since bronze has always been more highly thought of. But in the nineteenth century delicate *filigree* visiting-card cases of remarkably fine strands of silver (plate 58) were made for export, and small snuff- or trinket boxes, the

58.
Visiting-card case in silver filigree. Such card cases were not used in China; Chinese craftsmen made them for export to the West during the Victorian era. Chinese, nineteenth century. Height: 10 cm. (3⅞ in.). Cooper-Hewitt Museum, gift of Susan Dwight Bliss

latter often decorated with ivory portrait heads or cloisonné enamel, were quite common.

Pewter was popular. We know that it was being employed as early as the Han dynasty (221 B.C.–A.D. 220), although no early pewter boxes have been discovered. During the nineteenth century many were made both for home use and for export. These included subtle two- or three-compartment storage boxes with engraved decoration and champlevé enamel inlay (plate 59). Later pewter containers were also inlaid with bronze or studded with pieces of quartz, carnelian and the so-called Peking glass.

Brass has always been used in China. An alloy composed of two parts copper to one part zinc, it is hard, durable and takes on a sheen like gold. Chinese craftsmen have produced small fire boxes, or portable braziers, with pierced decoration; pill-, tinder- and cigarette boxes; and a variety of square or circular "notion" boxes set with semiprecious stones or cloisonné. Many of the early twentieth-century examples, marked CHINA, can be found in antiques shops today.

Copper is still popular for inexpensive wares such as pill- and cigarette boxes intended for the tourist trade; during the eighteenth and nineteenth centuries iron was employed for the extremely sophisticated money boxes and small chests used in Chinese homes and places of business.

59

60

Ivory and jade are held in particularly high regard. There is some evidence that elephants existed in China at the time the first civilizing influences arose there, and Chinese artisans certainly have a preference for elephant ivory. In the Ming era (1368–1644), Chinese expeditions to Southeast Asia were already bringing back tusks for carving. Over the years, these were made into boxes as well as all kinds of other objects. The Chinese ivory containers—for example, game-counter boxes and visiting-card cases (plate 60)—are carved with remarkable skill and clarity. Figures stand out in almost three-dimensional relief against a complex background. Such pieces may be tinted with pigments, but the majority are left in their natural hue.

Jade is the most highly treasured of all materials among the Chinese. Confucius (c. 551–479 B.C.) identified it with the cardinal virtues, declaring that the stone shone like benevolence, was strong and durable like wisdom, and like truth did not hide its flaws. A deep green to pale white mineral of great hardness, jade has long been imported from Burma and elsewhere since it is not found in China.

59.
Compartmented box, pewter engraved and inlaid in champlevé enamel. The Chinese are masters of enamelwork, which they have often combined with pewter and other metals. These boxes were made primarily for export to the West. Chinese, nineteenth century. Height: 8 cm. (3¼ in.). Metropolitan Museum of Art, New York, bequest of Dorothy Graham Bennett, 1959

60.
Visiting-card case, carved ivory. Ivory has a fine grain that lends itself to highly skilled and detailed carving. Chinese, nineteenth century. Height: 8.9 cm. (3½ in.). Cooper-Hewitt Museum, gift of Mrs. John Innes Kane from the estate of and in memory of Mrs. Samuel W. Brigham

Carved jade has been excavated from Chinese tombs of the pre-Christian era. But some fine examples were produced during the reign of the emperor Ch'ien-lung (1736–96). Because jade is so costly, containers of this material have tended to be small—dainty rouge boxes, match-safes or snuffboxes being most common.

Collectors of jade and ivory have to contend with a variety of fakes and reproductions. The stone may be dyed to give it a darker hue, or imitated by other minerals such as serpentine or soapstone, and even modern plastics. Molded plastic often passes for ivory as well, just as Celluloid once did.

Other semiprecious stones from which such boxes were carved include quartz, rock crystal, agate and lapis lazuli. All are materials of some value, and when finely worked have fetched substantial prices. Again, for the most part these pieces tend to be small.

The Chinese use the sap from the sumac, or *lacquer* tree (*Rhus verniciflua*), to create their highly prized lacquerwares, in which many coats of lacquer are applied to a wooden, paper or leather base. The screens are outstanding, but boxes and other objects were also made. Often the finish is gilded or inlaid with mother-of-pearl to heighten the luxuriant effect.

Lacquerware boxes have been found in tombs of the Han period, so there is no doubt that the art is an ancient one. Most common are painted lacquer toilet boxes and containers to hold tea, pins and sweetmeats. The famed Chinese coromandel work, begun in the seventeenth century, was used on some boxes. Here the surface is built up with designs of people and landscapes made by applying a claylike substance that is then carved and lacquered. Coromandel work is fragile, and good examples are much prized.

In cinnabar work, a lacquer surface is built up to sufficient height to be carved in low relief. Although the term specifically refers to the red or "cinnabar" color (colorplate 18), carved lacquer boxes are found in green, brown, black or purple, or combinations of these hues. Some of the most beautiful examples are those in which coats of contrasting colors were applied so that the craftsman could cut through the top layer to expose the variant hues below.

Probably the most famous Chinese boxes are those made of pottery and porcelain. The former are of natural clay as extracted from the ground; the latter of a precise mixture of kaolin and petuntse given a glaze resembling glass. A type of porcelain had already been developed in China by the seventh century.

Celadon, a blue-gray or green-gray glaze much prized for its resemblance to jade, must be the ware most closely associated with China in the minds of many connoisseurs. Celadon wares were being exported by the Chinese as far back as the Tang period (618–906), and early examples are much sought after, although boxes in this material are practically unobtainable today.

Colorplate 18.
Carved lacquer covered box. The emperor Yung-Lo so appreciated the art of lacquerwork that he invited artists to Peking to establish a factory that could provide wares for the imperial court. Chinese, Ming dynasty, Yung-Lo period (1403–25). Diameter: 26.6 cm. (10½ in.). Freer Gallery of Art

During the Ch'ing dynasty (1644–1912) Chinese potters developed a thriving trade with the West, exporting vast quantities of porcelain. Groups of stacking boxes and tea caddies were among the larger items, along with the usual sweetmeat boxes, pin and cigarette containers, as well as a host of other intriguing but unidentifiable pieces. Most looked like boxes; but some were shaped like birds (particularly ducks), shellfish (plate 61), even human beings.

These porcelain pieces were generally attractive in form, but their color and decoration were what caught the collector's eye. The stark blue-and-white landscapes or rich floral compositions in shades of pink, blue, green, yellow and orange are equally striking. Such surfaces were achieved in one of two ways. The popular blue-and-white Canton and Nanking wares were embellished by a design painted directly onto the clay, then dipped in a clear glaze and fired—a technique known as underglaze. Since only certain blue and red colorants could stand the high temperatures required to fire porcelain, underglaze was limited to these two colors.

To obtain a broader palette, the Chinese would first bake the clear glazed piece, then apply enamels that could be "set," or hardened, by reheating the piece at a lower temperature. This technique is known as overglaze decoration. The majority of nineteenth- and twentieth-

61.
Box in the form of a crab, polychrome porcelain. The Chinese delighted in creating delicate china boxes in unexpected forms such as shellfish, flowers and animals. Chinese, nineteenth century. Length: 16.5 cm. (6½ in.). Metropolitan Museum of Art, New York, purchase by subscription, 1879

century porcelain boxes available today have been decorated in the overglaze manner.

Finally, Chinese boxes in such natural materials as tortoiseshell (plate 62) or wood, often inlaid with soapstone, brass or semiprecious stones, are occasionally found.

62.
Round covered box, shaped and carved tortoiseshell. When first dampened and then heated, tortoiseshell can be pressed into various forms and decorated with carving. Chinese, eighteenth century. Diameter: 7.1 cm. (2⅞ in.). Metropolitan Museum of Art, New York, bequest of Mary Stillman Harkness, 1950

Korea Korea adjoins China on the north and has for centuries been under the cultural, if not the outright political and economic, domination of its larger neighbor. Korean boxes tend to resemble those made in China both in their form and in the materials employed.

Bronze boxes are rare and precious in Korea, but other metalwork is more easily obtainable. Finely crafted iron boxes inlaid with silver (plate 63) have been produced for generations, as have containers in brass. Wood is used to great effect, frequently inlaid with brass, silver or iron. Although most Korean boxes of this sort are small, some are large enough to be classified as chests.

The Koreans have produced lacquerware boxes, often employing a technique known in the West as "lac burgauté," whereby tortoiseshell, animal bone or mother-of-pearl is carefully inlaid into the lacquered surface. Such pieces sometimes resemble Chinese examples from the Tang period, reflecting the prevailing influence of the dominant culture.

Best known of the limited quantity of Korean pottery is celadon ware. The boxes made during the Koryo dynasty (918–1392) are particularly prized for their delicacy and their fine color (colorplate 19).

63

Colorplate 19.
Cosmetic box with inlaid slip decoration, celadon. Korean celadon ware is limited in quantity but among the finest ever produced. Korean, Koryo dynasty, twelfth century. Diameter: 8.1 cm. (3⅛ in.). Freer Gallery of Art

63.
Storage box, wrought iron inlaid with silver. Although related to Chinese examples, Korean metalwork has its own national character. Korean, seventeenth century. Length: 10.5 cm. (4⅛ in.). Metropolitan Museum of Art, New York, Rogers Fund, 1922

Japan The Japanese were greatly influenced by Chinese styles and techniques. But partly as a result of their more isolated location and partly because they retained their political independence, the craftsmen of Japan evolved unique interpretations of themes prevalent on the mainland. Their bronzes provide a good example. The Japanese were making cast-bronze objects by the Asuka era (c. A.D. 450) that are reminiscent in form of the Chinese examples. But whereas the Chinese decorated their pieces with highly stylized designs, the Japanese chose to cover the surfaces of their boxes, bells and mirrors with hunting scenes or depictions of birds and animals native to the islands. This interest in genre, the life of the commonplace, has continued to be characteristic of Japanese taste in every field of the decorative arts.

Most Japanese bronzes that are available today, including boxes, date from the nineteenth century. At this time, native craftsmen turned out large numbers of pieces in an archaic Chinese style, which they coated with dark brown lacquer to create the appearance of great age. More than one enthusiast has been fooled by what appears to be a very old "Chinese" box but is in actuality a Japanese example made in the 1880s.

The Japanese lacked the Chinese reverence for bronze; indeed, they have always preferred working in iron, an art at which they have long excelled. Although their swords are justly famous, many small containers (plate 64) have been made, including square tobacco boxes and braziers, snuff- and matchboxes, and the small pill or seal containers known as *inro*.

Usually no more than three inches long and two inches wide, inro were little boxes divided into compartments and used (in place of pockets) to hold personal items such as medicines, perfumes, signature

64.
Casket or storage box in the shape of a woven basket, wrought iron. Although some of the finest iron work by Japanese craftsmen appears on swords and armor, they also made a wide variety of iron boxes and other objects. Japanese, seventeenth century. Length: 23.5 cm. (9¼ in.). Metropolitan Museum of Art, New York, gift of Howard Mansfield, 1936

seals and ink. They were fastened to the belt that bound the kimono by an even smaller toggle called a netsuke.

Made in other materials as well as bronze, inro were intricately carved, lacquered or inlaid, and frequently boasted a complete miniature landscape on the surface, perhaps signed by a well-known artist (see frontispiece). The better inro are obviously much sought after, but it is still possible to obtain reasonable late-nineteenth- and twentieth-century examples.

Although undertaken at a relatively late date, during the 1830s, the technique of cloisonné became in the hands of the Japanese a fine art. Their cloisonné boxes come in varied shapes—and range in size from miniature round or oblong pillboxes to the large multi-unit stacking boxes used to carry food. Japanese cloisonné can often be distinguished from its Chinese counterpart by the treatment of the background. Characteristically, this is left unpatterned, whereas Chinese examples are filled with stylized patterns resembling thunderclouds, fretwork, and the like.

On a less obvious and more sophisticated level, the Japanese craftsmen developed a variety of transparent enamels applied over silver or gold foil to create a spectacular arrangement that often seems to float in the air rather than be affixed to the metal or ceramic base. Another distinctive element of the Japanese work is its design. Japanese boxes frequently feature highly naturalistic renditions of landscapes, flowers and street scenes, topics dear to this people but of little interest to the Chinese cloisonné artists.

The best of Japanese work will often bear the mark of its creator. Less important examples, like the Japanese ceramics and bronzes made for export, may bear pseudo-Chinese reign marks to complete the work of copying.

Inro and small containers to hold pills or breath sweeteners, lighting materials and tobacco or visiting cards (plate 65) were sometimes made of silver, although such examples are uncommon. There is a fair amount of inexpensive Japanese brass and copper, most of it produced since 1900 in the form of cigarette and matchboxes and similar objects intended to be sold to the same foreign markets at which comparable Chinese items were directed. While plentiful, such pieces are seldom of any great quality.

Among natural materials, the Japanese have long excelled in boxes carved out of wood and ivory. Most characteristic of all are the bamboo pieces. Delicate needle holders and brush receptacles are made from sections of the tall, knobby plant. Wood such as pine and spruce may be shaped into lunch or carrying boxes—picnic boxes in the West—which are decorated with painted devices or inlaid with pewter, porcelain or mother-of-pearl much like similar Chinese containers.

65.
Visiting-card case, repoussé silver in a floral pattern with touches of polychrome enamel. Japanese metalsmiths often combined silver with enamel. Japanese, nineteenth century. Height: 9.3 cm. (3⅝ in.). Cooper-Hewitt Museum, gift of Mr. and Mrs. Maxime Hermanos

As ivory carvers, the Japanese are equal to the Chinese, although here too their products have a unique national quality. Chinese boxes in this medium tend to be decorated with slender figures of classical origin—Taoist Immortals, Buddhist deities, and so on. The Japanese examples are much more naturalistic; containers may be carved in relief with a village scene, a grasshopper (or even *in* the form of a grasshopper) or a scene from a historical period or a famous Kabuki play.

As small as they were, inro made of ivory were often carved and incised with elaborately detailed scenes that were recognized as works of art. Renowned artists in much larger mediums, such as Korin (1658–1716) and Zeshin (1807–1891), were proud to work on these small surfaces. Inro were made from a number of different materials, including lacquerware, metal and even carved fruit pits; but many of the most charming are of ivory, in most cases from the walrus rather than the elephant. The art of inro making is still extant and examples by respected contemporary carvers bring high prices. Craftsmen in this field frequently sign their works.

Somewhat larger ivory boxes were used to hold pins, game counters, cigarettes and snuff. Many were made for export, and it should be noted that, like the Chinese, Japanese manufacturers over half a century ago were using wax or Celluloid to imitate ivory. (The

66.
Game box, teakwood inlaid with ivory, and carved ivory figures. The counters are in the form of masks used by characters in the popular Noh plays. Japanese, nineteenth century. Diameter: 11.4 cm. (4½ in.). Cooper-Hewitt Museum, gift of Susan Dwight Bliss

addition of modern plastics has presented the collector with further problems of identification.)

Craftsmen often combined ivory with wood. Carved ivory game figures may be enclosed in a box of teak or spruce, the exterior of which is embellished with applied figures or abstract devices again carved out of ivory (plate 66).

The art of making lacquerware was brought from China to Japan during the Tang era (618–906) and took firm hold in the island nation. Since so many layers of lacquer must be laid over the base material and the decorative work must be done while the medium is still damp, lacquerware is best made in a humid climate. Japan, which is moist and foggy much of the year, proved a very suitable location for the craft. In fact, so skilled did the artisans there become that by the fifteenth century Chinese workmen were journeying to Japan to learn the new techniques practiced in its workshops.

Japanese lacquerwares generally fall into two categories. First are the plain examples in one or two colors on a traditional wooden base (plate 67). These reflect the continuation of an early preference for the traditional and highly stylized work produced in China. On the other hand, the Japanese did not hesitate to experiment with decorative techniques, materials and forms; as a result, their lacquerware tradition is considerably more complex than that of China.

While wood has always been the material on which most lacquer bodies are formed, the Japanese have employed other mediums, including leather, bamboo, cloth and even paper. As early as the Heian period (898–1185), lacquerware boxes decorated with mother-of-pearl were being made to house a range of items from cosmetics to the Buddhist sutra. It is not at all unusual for this work to combine lacquer with such diverse elements as silver, brass, ivory, seashells and mother-of-pearl (colorplate 20 and plate 68).

As in the case of other artistic mediums, the Japanese preferred earthy and naturalistic themes to the more abstract and ethereal ones favored by Chinese artisans. Highly realistic flowers are a popular choice, particularly for boxes to be used by women, and a larger piece may be decorated with a lifelike rendition of ships and sea birds (plate 69), Samurai in battle or Geisha playing musical instruments.

The finest Japanese lacquerwares date from the Kamakura (1185–1333) and the Edo (1615–1868) periods; many of the magnificent lacquer inro were produced during the latter era. However, the craft is far from lost, and a great many lacquered boxes have been made in the past century. Most of these are rather ordinary, intended primarily for sale as inexpensive tourist items, but some work of very high-quality has been achieved. The better-grade items are often signed by the artist.

Although they had made earthenware pottery for centuries, the islanders did not develop a porcelain industry until the sixteenth

67.
Tea box (natsume) with cover in brown, gold and silver lacquer over wood. Japan's damp climate was particularly well suited to the production of lacquerwares because the lacquer remained soft for the period necessary to complete the work. Japanese, nineteenth century. Height: 5.9 cm. (2⅜ in.). Cooper-Hewitt Museum, anonymous gift

68.
Box for letters, lacquered wood with brass and silver. The traditional fu-bako, or letter box, was often made of lacquerware. Japanese, early nineteenth century. Length: 24.4 cm. (9⅝ in.). Cooper-Hewitt Museum, gift of Mr. and Mrs. Maxime Hermanos

Colorplate 20.
Rectangular covered box, lacquered wood with silver, mother-of-pearl, ivory and seashells. The beautiful, shimmering surface of this box has been created by layering intricately carved mother-of-pearl flowers on a lacquer surface. Japanese, attributed to the artist Yeki-ko, nineteenth century. Length: 9.8 cm. (3⅞ in.). Cooper-Hewitt Museum, anonymous gift

69.
Smoking cabinet or box in lacquered wood with brass and silver accessories. Pipehooks swing out from the corners of this elaborate chest, which was used for storing tobacco and smoking implements. Japanese, nineteenth century. Length: 25.2 cm. (10 in.). Cooper-Hewitt Museum, gift of Mr. and Mrs. Maxime Hermanos

Colorplate 21.
Incense box in the form of a rabbit, earthenware. Figural containers are among the most interesting of Japanese boxes. Japanese, attributed to Ninsei, seventeenth century. Height: 8.2 cm. (3¼ in.). Freer Gallery of Art

70.
Sectional porcelain box, Nabeshima ware. In the style of the potter Sakaida Kakiemon, this miniature piece typifies the high-quality wares produced in Japan's Hizen Province. Japanese, 1750. Height: 5.7 cm. (2¼ in.). Metropolitan Museum of Art, New York, gift of Charles Stewart Smith, 1893

century, long after they had learned of the translucent ceramic from their mainland neighbors. Some scholars feel that this delay reflects the great love the Japanese felt for their lacquerware.

Once they began to make porcelain, however, the Japanese excelled in the field. Some of their loveliest ceramic boxes were made for export at Arita on the island of Kyushu and shipped from the local port of Imari. *Imari* ware is lavishly decorated, embellished with borders slip-painted to look like silk brocade, and figures of fish, flowers and people in red, green and orange highlighted by gilded areas and a strong blue-black ground. It proved so popular an export that the Chinese themselves copied the type. Nabeshima ware was once produced solely for the feudal lords of Arita. Although found on boxes in different color combinations, Nabeshima ware is best known in a rich blue on a white ground (plate 70).

Three other well-known ceramic wares in which containers have been produced are Satsuma, Kakiemon and Kutani. The eighteenth- and early-nineteenth-century examples include few boxes—a cosmetic box or two and the occasional tea canister, little more. But once Japan began making porcelain for collectors in the late nineteenth century, new forms appeared. These pin, cigarette and sundries boxes are often found with the marks of Nippon or Japan—a requirement of American import laws.

Japanese earthenware also comes in great variety. Boxes in this medium may be easily recognizable as containers or may be disguised as animals (colorplate 21), flowers or natural objects, such as trees or rocks.

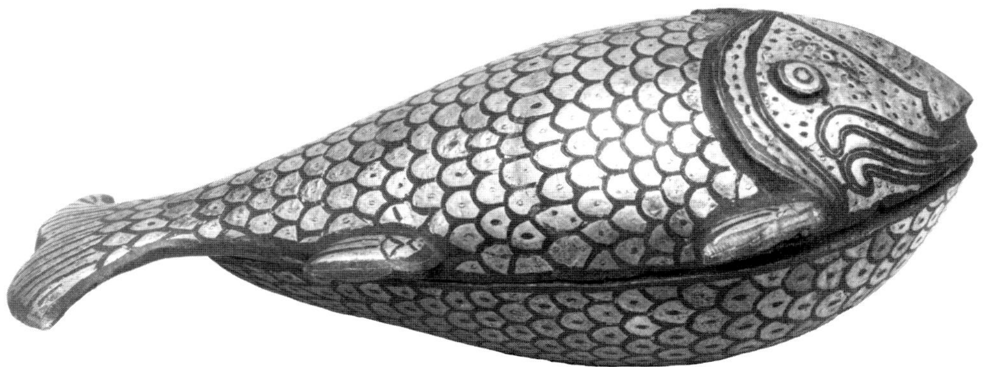

71.
Box, perhaps a perfume holder, cast pewter inlaid with silver. Known as Bidri ware, Indian pewter is found in unusual and appealing forms. Indian, Lucknow, nineteenth century. Length: 22.9 cm. (9 in.). Metropolitan Museum of Art, New York, gift of Robert W. and Lockwood DeForest, 1919

72.
Miniature box, gold decorated in champlevé enamel (foreground), with hand-embroidered case. Little more than an inch square, this piece illustrates the remarkable ability of Indian craftsmen to create detail in miniature. Indian, nineteenth century. Height: 2.8 cm. (1⅛ in.). Cooper-Hewitt Museum, anonymous gift

India India is the other great boxmaking center of the East. Native craftsmen have proven particularly proficient in producing small containers, above all in metal. Copper and brass have long been worked in India. The Punjab area is noted for its copper-gilt toilet boxes with their remarkably ornate locks, and the Moradabad and Hyderabad areas for their brass wares. Boxes from the Punjab are decorated with complex engravings, while examples from Hyderabad generally are inlaid in copper. Many of these containers, made during the nineteenth century, were destined for export and bear the mark INDIA or some variant thereof.

Less often seen in collections or shops are examples of Indian pewter work. For over two hundred years skilled workers in the town of Bidar have made boxes and other utensils that are cast in molds, then finished on a lathe, and often inlaid with silver or gold in floral and geometric patterns. Known as Bidri ware, these containers are

72

frequently cast in the form of fish (plate 71) or animals.

Cloisonné, too, was practiced on the great subcontinent. Generally worked on a copper or brass base, Indian cloisonné is characterized by its bold colors and by the use of motifs—birds, fish and so on—that have been adapted from the miniature painting for which the country is so well known. A great variety of fine cloisonné enamel is still exported; cigarette and matchboxes, jewel and pillboxes are particularly popular.

Examples in more valuable materials are far less common. A few Indian boxes in silver are available, and gold boxes are known, but traditionally the use of precious metals was restricted to royalty, so containers in this medium were never plentiful. Indian artisans customarily decorated their gold pieces with red and green enamels (plate 72) and their silver pieces with blue and green.

While never as highly prized as it was in China, jade was regarded as a precious stone in India and was often used for containers needed in religious rites or those for the storage of precious jewels. The jade jewel boxes were frequently further encrusted with diamonds, rubies or sapphires, and bound with bands of gold (plate 73).

Ivory was employed, both for small boxes carved of the material and as inlay in larger containers, usually of wood. Indian inlay work in ivory is of the highest quality. Tiny pieces are fitted together to create remarkably elaborate floral patterns that may often cover much of the surface of the box they decorate (plate 74). Some such pieces are still made for export, but they lack the quality of nineteenth-century examples, and plastic is sometimes substituted for ivory.

73.
Jewel casket, white jade ornamented with gold, rubies, emeralds, diamonds and sapphires. Indian jewel boxes were often further embellished with jewels. Indian, nineteenth century. Length: 16.2 cm. (6⅜ in.). Metropolitan Museum of Art, New York, Sylmaris Collection, gift of George Coe Graves, 1930

74

Tibet Bordered by both India and China, Tibet has produced boxes that bear stylistic similarities to those of its neighbors. Most existent examples are in base metal and include perfume, charm and sundries containers. But the finest boxes are of silver. These are characterized by their excellent engraving and by the masterful use of applied decorative elements (plate 75).

Being relatively hard to obtain in Tibet, silver was by tradition used primarily for the royal classes and religious orders while the

74.
Storage box, wood inlaid in ivory. Indian inlay work frequently includes elaborate floral patterns. Indian, seventeenth century. Length: 54.9 cm. (21⅝ in.). Metropolitan Museum of Art, New York, Fletcher Fund, 1976

75.
Charm box, silver with applied semiprecious stones. Tibetan silver often comes in small but elaborate forms. The presence of the ring on this piece suggests that it may have been intended to be hung from a belt or necklace. Tibetan, eighteenth century. Height: 14.6 cm. (5¾ in.). Metropolitan Museum of Art, New York, Rogers Fund, 1916

75

76.
Covered box, bronze embellished with colored stones. Like their Chinese neighbors, the Tibetans have worked in bronze for centuries. Tibetan, eighteenth century. Diameter: 24.1 cm. (9½ in.). Metropolitan Museum of Art, New York, bequest of Collis P. Huntington, 1925

general citizenry made do with containers in bronze. Small covered boxes decorated with colored stones or glass (plate 76) were produced in limited quantity. Some work exists in brass and iron as well as in such natural materials as wood (often inlaid in brass or cut stone), jade and ivory. For the most part, available examples date to the late nineteenth or early twentieth century.

The Pacific Islands The island cultures of the Pacific have not produced as many box types, nor have they used as many different materials, as on the mainland. Nevertheless, interesting things can be found. Indonesia and the Philippine Islands, the major landmasses in the area and the ones most subject to foreign influences, offer the greatest variety. Indonesia has become noted for its brightly painted boxes of wood, often inlaid with mother-of-pearl and various seashells. The Philippines are home to craftsmen who manufacture several characteristic kinds of containers.

In those areas where the Spanish influence was prevalent, delicate silver filigree cigarette boxes and card cases, modeled on Iberian types, were and still are made. In many of the southern Philippine islands the Muslim influence was considerable, and metal boxes clearly related to those manufactured in the Near East have been found. Most of these are of brass or pewter and fall into two distinct types. First are the cast and hammer-shaped boxes inlaid with abstract floral motifs in pewter (plate 77). These have hinged lids and may be square, rectangular or octagonal in shape. The second type consists of rectangular storage boxes of brass, decorated with complex wire decoration laid down in arabesques, again a distinctly Islamic style (plate 78). Both types are made by the Moro people of the islands adjoining the Sulu Sea and are becoming harder to find as these relatively primitive groups integrate further into the Philippine culture.

The small island cultures of Micronesia, Melanesia and Polynesia have left comparatively few containers, mostly of painted and carved wood. Due to the disastrous effects of European contact on these peoples, such boxes do not usually date after 1900, and today the craft is essentially lost. Yet museums and private collections contain enough examples to indicate that boxmaking was once an important art in these areas.

Boxes to hold betel nuts, lime, fish hooks, food and holy objects were all made. The finest examples, manufactured by the Maori people of New Zealand, show a sophistication and abstraction of design equal to that achieved in many more "civilized" areas of the world. Maori boxes, such as the Waka Huia, or treasure boxes, and the long, cigar-shaped containers intended for the storage of feathers (plate 79), had surfaces completely covered with shallow carving in curvilinear elements. Such carving was related to the tattoos with which people adorned their bodies. These boxes, though relatively small, are quite remarkably detailed.

77.
Covered box, brass inlaid with pewter, with a cloth carrying strap. Skillfully inlaid pewter creates a stencil-like effect on this box. Philippine, Moro culture, nineteenth century. Length: 16.8 cm. (6⅝ in.). Cooper-Hewitt Museum, gift of Mr. and Mrs. Maxime Hermanos

78

78.
Covered box, brass decorated with applied brass wire decoration. The design of this piece clearly reflects Near Eastern influence. Philippine, Moro culture, nineteenth century. Length: 17.5 cm. (6⅞ in.). Cooper-Hewitt Museum, gift of Mr. and Mrs. Maxime Hermanos

79.
Box to hold feathers, carved wood. The carved heads at either end were used to secure cords for lifting the treasure up to the rafters for safekeeping. Melanesia, New Zealand, probably Maori, nineteenth to early twentieth century. Length: 47.6 cm. (18¾ in.). Metropolitan Museum, New York, Michael C. Rockefeller Memorial Collection, bequest of Nelson A. Rockefeller, 1979

79

COLORPLATE 22

COLORPLATE 23

6 Boxes of the Americas

Since the culture of North America was closely related to that of Europe, the early products of colonial and post-colonial craftsmen were akin to those made in the mother countries. However, the Indians and the Eskimos, who occupied areas eventually taken over by European settlers, created containers that were not only different in appearance and construction but also in purpose; much of their work reflected religious beliefs quite different from those held by the newcomers.

In the southern hemisphere, ancient and persistent native cultures came into even stronger conflict with European explorers and colonizers whose religious and political beliefs mandated the destruction of local social patterns. Most of the boxes indigenous to this area have been destroyed, and it would be difficult to put together a representative collection.

North America The majority of North American boxes—and the oldest—are of wood. Timber was abundant in the New World, and coopers were listed among the passengers on the earliest incoming ships, including the *Mayflower*. These craftsmen and the men they trained tended to follow European methods of boxmaking.

The earliest pioneer containers were quite primitive in appearance, which is not surprising considering the difficult conditions under which they were made and their highly functional purpose—to preserve precious items such as salt and candles from damp and rodents. Carved out of oak, often with pine tops or lids and bottoms, they were generally decorated with incised designs, pinwheels, hearts, stars and various geometric patterns, as well as having notched or chip-carved corners (plate 80). Such boxes were usually rather shallow, being intended primarily to store books, chiefly the Bible, which

Colorplate 22.
Lift-top storage box, polychrome painted pine. The patriotic fervor of the early nineteenth century led to the manufacture of many boxes and other objects embellished with symbols such as the eagle and the American flag. American, early nineteenth century. Length: 37.7 cm. (14⅞ in.). Museum of American Folk Art, Morris and Eva Feld Folk Art Acquisition Fund

Colorplate 23.
Trinket or storage box, wood decorated with paint, with pen and pencil drawings on paper set under glass panels. Pieces such as this are classified as folk art. Very often the scenes depicted on these boxes are related to events in the life of the maker. New England, c. 1825. Length: 20.3 cm. (8 in.). Museum of American Folk Art, purchase

80.
Desk or bible box, carved oak with pine top. Simple boxes like this were used for storing important papers or the family Bible, often the only book in the house. American, c. 1675–1700. Length: 65.6 cm. (26¼ in.). Metropolitan Museum of Art, New York, gift of Mrs. Russell Sage, 1909

81.
Double-pedestal box, chip-carved decoration. Made from cedar cigar boxes, this piece is in the style termed tramp art, although few such examples were actually made by itinerants. American, late nineteenth to early twentieth century. Length: 35.6 cm. (14 in.). Private collection

82.
Set of oval "nesting" pantry boxes, birch with pine tops and bottoms. These containers were made by the Shakers, a religious group whose members were skilled craftsmen. American, nineteenth century. Length of largest box: 34.3 cm. (13½ in.). Hancock Shaker Village/Shaker Community, Pittsfield, Massachusetts

was often the only volume to be found in the home. The term *bible box* is frequently applied to them, while similar examples made with sloping lids were used as writing boxes.

The technique of gouge or chip carving as a decorative device died out in America soon after 1700, but it was revived almost two hundred years later when amateur wood workers began to make what is now known as tramp art. These pieces, which range from picture frames to elaborate boxes (plate 81) and even furniture, were assembled from scrapwood (usually cigar boxes or fruit crates), cut to shape on a jig saw, then covered with layers of complex gouge carving. Most tramp art is painted in one or more colors; some examples are decorated with bits of colored glass, beads and so on. Unlike the early gouge-carved containers, which are hard to find and expensive, tramp art is readily available to the collector. Trinket, vanity, storage, cigarette and jewelry boxes are among the forms encountered.

Related to such pieces are the small and rather clever spruce gum boxes that were carved by loggers and woodsmen in New England and eastern Canada around the period 1875 to 1930. Unlike tramp art boxes, these containers tended to take a specific form, that of a small book with a sliding cover. Most were carved from a single block of pine, fir or spruce, and were decorated with shallow chip carving that might or might not include painted embellishment. Made primarily as rustic gifts for loved ones, the boxes frequently were filled with spruce gum, the chewable pitch of the spruce tree.

Other craftsmen also made boxes in the shape of books, intended primarily to house books and papers. These were usually larger, painted and made from several pieces of wood nailed or dovetailed together. They are not common.

By the end of the eighteenth century painting had almost entirely replaced carving as the means of decorating boxes. Such decoration reflected the worker's skill and the materials available to him, and also in some cases the stylistic period in which he worked. But most of the professional craftsmen, the so-called white coopers, who turned out containers both large and small,wasted little time on decoration unless it was paid for; their standard product was most often left completely undecorated, or else just varnished or given a simple coat of solid red, blue or green.

These containers did get decorated further, though—by the men, women or children who purchased them and then carefully covered their surfaces with everything from simple black splotches on a red ground (termed *spongework*) to highly sophisticated art. Many were made during the period from 1800 to 1850, when the nation was expanding, and they reflect the general feeling of well-being. Boxes with eagles (colorplate 22), cornucopias, American flags and similar motifs are not uncommon, although simple renditions of flowers, trees, houses and animals (colorplate 23) occur rather more often.

The majority of the better-decorated containers are low, rectangular pieces generally known as toilet or dressing boxes, and eight-sided examples termed trinket boxes. By this period toilet boxes were normally owned and used by women, some of whom may have decorated their own.

81

82

Not all of these containers were simply hand-painted. Some were decorated with the use of stencils; later in the nineteenth century others were covered with bits of cutout paper, a technique known as *decoupage*. Decoupage actually developed from an earlier art, known as potichomania, practiced in France in the mid-nineteenth century. This involved the pasting of brightly colored scraps of paper inside a glass vessel or onto the back of a piece of glass in imitation of porcelain. Potichomania became so popular in the 1860s that factories were turning out sheets of paper with pictures and motifs in such varied modes as Chinese figures and Dresden medallions.

In the United States, although potichomania was used, women (for it was primarily a woman's hobby) soon found that it was much easier to glue the pictures and other scraps cut from illustrated magazines to the outside of their bottles, glasses and containers. A coat of varnish was applied to preserve the surface, and the finished product became an art object for display on table or mantel. Decoupage was popular in North America for several decades, being practiced on everything from the usual bottles and pottery jugs to chairs covered with postage stamps.

Sophisticated boxes of the same period were inlaid in satinwood or boxwood, and might be *veneered* in curly maple or flame mahogany over a pine carcass. They are usually in the later Federal or the Empire style, although a few equally lavish Victorian examples may be found. Sometimes gilded and adorned with brass handles and other accessories, they were quite large. The most common forms were lift-top writing boxes; lap desks to hold ink bottles, pens and other appropriate materials; and trinket and toilet boxes.

Most workaday boxes were not nearly so glamorous. Throughout the past two hundred years coopers and later small woodenware factories have turned out receptacles of all kinds for use in the home and shop. Although generally undecorated or simply painted, these boxes are often of great interest to collectors simply because of their role in American home and work life. For example, the bee box, a wood and glass container with sliding lid and two compartments, was designed to capture and transport the queen bee (and hence the hive). The dough box, a rectangular covered container, was for storing and working bread dough. And a long, slim, straight box held razors. Ballot boxes came with slots in the lid for the casting of votes, money boxes with compartmented interiors and oval spectacle boxes with interiors carved in the shape of eyeglasses; small tobacco boxes were often decorated with sliding tops.

All these containers were normally nailed or dovetailed together or, like the small cylindrical needle and toothpick boxes, turned on a lathe. A few required carving, but most could be put together rather quickly.

Another very large group of wooden containers was made by soaking strips of thin birch, ash or other flexible wood until they were soft enough to be bent around oval or round pine tops and bottoms, then nailed or pegged into place. Most such pieces were termed pantry or spice boxes, and they were customarily made in small shops where they could be shaped over wooden molds or forms of appropriate sizes.

Pantry boxes could be used to store sugar, flour and other dry goods in bulk, while spice boxes served to protect herbs and spices. A third category, the cheese box, is still used to store and ship cheese. All three types came in varying sizes, ranging from a few inches for the spices to cheese containers that were two feet long. It was also common to make a particular box form in several sizes so that they might be stacked one within the other, or "nested."

Nests of boxes are referred to in seventeenth-century American estate inventories. But it is generally agreed that the finest nesting boxes are those produced in the nineteenth and early twentieth centuries by the craftsmen of the Shaker religious sect, which was active in much of the Northeast and parts of the Midwest and South from the 1790s until well into this century. Shaker boxes could be used to safeguard everything from medicines and buttons to starched collars. They were generally oval in shape, and had tapering "laps," or fingers, that were secured by wooden pins, lead, iron or copper nails or by rivets (plate 82). These boxes were originally left in their natural finish, or at most given just a thin wash of blue, yellow, red or green paint. Their simplicity of line and fine quality of construction—combined with the Shakers' keen awareness of detail—have won the hearts of many collectors.

Men and women used bandboxes, sometimes of wood but more often of cardboard, to carry around various articles of clothing and small accessories. References to these receptacles also appear in seventeenth-century inventories, and throughout the eighteenth and the first half of the nineteenth centuries they seem to have been exceedingly common. A few were made by individual craftspersons, such as Hannah Davis (1784–1863) of Jaffrey, New Hampshire, who built up a fine reputation for her work. But most were produced by factories that also made wallpaper, a natural combination since most bandboxes are covered with wallpaper. Indeed, the decorations on the paper (colorplate 24) are one of the main reasons for current interest in the form. Bright flowers, exotic birds and views of public buildings such as New York's City Hall grace many of these otherwise rather ordinary containers.

Hats and combs were stored in boxes made of cardboard or wood covered with colored paper. The early men's hatboxes were triangular to accommodate the hats worn then, but at a later date they

Colorplate 24

Colorplate 25

became rounded like bandboxes. The large ivory, horn and tortoiseshell combs worn by women in the early nineteenth century were stored in striking demilune-shaped containers.

Later, in the second half of the century, paper and cardboard boxes were extensively used to package commercial products, including tobacco, food and various dry goods. All such boxes are considered collectible if the colored lithography on them is interesting enough. Collectors are especially attracted to the large, flat boxes in which games were sold. Known as board games because they were customarily played on a piece of cardboard on which the course had been laid out, these amusements were almost a mania among Victorians of all ages and remain popular today. Parker Brothers and W. & S. B. Ives, both of Salem, Massachusetts, produced thousands of different games; the colorful boxes in which they were stored are collected and even mounted like prints or pictures.

Most bride's boxes identified as American have come from the Pennsylvania area, where the Germanic settlers followed Old World traditions in their making and presentation. These large oval containers, usually of bentwood, brightly decorated with flowers and figures, often look so much like the more numerous central European ones that collectors must exercise great caution in ascertaining their origin.

The development in the late nineteenth century of modern industrial processes led to a general decline in the art of making wooden boxes. But some fine pieces continued to appear in this medium, including typically individualistic examples by Louis Comfort Tiffany (1848–1933) (plate 83).

Decorated tin boxes were made in large quantities from the 1820s to the close of the nineteenth century. These were characteristically rectangular, with domed or flat tops, and were used primarily to store papers, hence the term document box. Examples that have a black or red ground upon which brightly painted designs appear (plate 84) are known as toleware; today they are considered of great interest and bring high prices.

Iron and brass have been used for cash boxes; tin was also employed for round or square tinderboxes in which materials to start a fire were stored. The dainty silver snuffboxes produced in such quantity in Europe were seldom made in America, but in the late nineteenth and early twentieth centuries American manufacturers turned out small storage boxes and containers in silver and electroplate to hold ladies' trinkets and visiting cards and men's cigars and cigarettes. Bronze was occasionally used, as was pewter, but containers in these materials are not common. Gold is more often found as embellishment to a box in another medium (colorplate 25) than as the sole material.

The art of *scrimshaw*, or of ivory carving, was practiced by American sailors throughout most of the last century (plate 85). Typically, a pattern was laid out on the surface to be decorated by

Colorplate 24.
Bandbox, cardboard covered with printed wallpaper including a depiction of a woman in a Roman chariot. These boxes were used to store and carry hats, gloves, starched and pleated collars, cuffs, neckbands and so on. American, c. 1830. Height: 36 cm. (14½ in.). Cooper-Hewitt Museum, gift of Mrs. James O. Green

Colorplate 25.
Oblong box with hinged lid, opal matrix set with diamonds and emeralds, gold and silver gilt. American boxes of this quality compare favorably with those being made in Europe at the same time. American, c. 1900–1920. Length: 10 cm. (4 in.). Cooper-Hewitt Museum, gift of Susan Dwight Bliss

83

83.
Covered box in naturalistic form, wood carved and decorated with glass scarabs. This unusual container was designed by Louis Comfort Tiffany (1848–1933), the famous glassmaker. American, late nineteenth to early twentieth century. Height: 11.4 cm. (4½ in.). Metropolitan Museum of Art, New York, gift of Hugh Grant, 1974

84.
Two dome-top document boxes, painted tin. Toleware was sold by itinerant traders throughout the eastern United States. American, first half of the nineteenth century. Length of larger box: 30.5 cm. (12 in.). Private collection

following the outline of a picture cut from a magazine such as *Godey's Lady's Book.* The incised picture was then filled in with lamp black or ink. Scrimshaw work is very popular with collectors and quite expensive, but inevitably extensive reproduction and faking have ensued.

Other natural materials include tortoiseshell, mother-of-pearl (plate 86), hide and leather. During the Victorian era and well into the twentieth century, factories produced card cases and powder boxes of tortoiseshell. Today the fear that the great turtles will become extinct has led to laws forbidding the use of tortoiseshell, and such objects are now made from a plastic substitute. Mother-of-pearl is still available and still used in box manufacture.

Throughout much of the last century one of the traveler's constant companions was the hide box or trunk. Made of wood covered with calfskin secured and decorated with brass tacks, these containers shed water and were surprisingly sturdy. Many are still available to collectors. In the southwestern United States Spanish-Americans wove strands of cowhide into small leather boxes. The work was done while the leather was wet; when dry, the containers proved both attractive and durable (plate 87).

Horn—usually cow horn—was also used. Sections of cut horn were plugged at each end to make small snuff containers or the larger holders for gunpowder. As horn provides a good surface for incised decoration, many of these pieces were covered with geometric designs, some of which were also colored with ink or oil-based colors.

Ceramic containers were relatively uncommon in America until the late nineteenth century, when the development of sophisticated casting procedures heralded a modern clay-working industry. Then

84

85

86

87

85.
Storage or "ditty" box, carved and engraved baleen and whalebone. Making boxes for loved ones was a traditional sailor's pastime. American, New England, mid-nineteenth century. Height: 5.8 cm. (2 in.). Private collection

86.
Visiting-card case, mother-of-pearl, carved and pierced. Very popular with Victorian Americans, card cases came in many different materials. American, c. 1850–53. Height: 9.1 cm. (3⅝ in.). Cooper-Hewitt Museum, gift of Mrs. Charles W. Lester

87.
Covered box, rawhide and leather lined with cloth. The Spanish-American settlers of Arizona and New Mexico produced boxes that harkened back to old Spain. Southwestern United States, late nineteenth century. Length: 20.3 cm. (8 in.). Private collection

88.
Hen on nest, brown-glazed white earthenware. This box, made by Hull Pottery Company in Crooksville, Ohio, is in a form that has been traditional for boxes and other containers since the early nineteenth century. American, twentieth century. Height: 11.8 cm. (4¾ in.). Private collection

manufacturers turned out quantities of pottery and porcelain boxes, most of them modeled on European examples but lacking the same sophistication. Some came in the shapes of hens (plate 88), dogs or other animals, houses and even motor cars; such receptacles continue to be popular today.

American craftsmen developed the process of glass pressing in the 1820s, and thereafter large quantities of pressed glass were produced by factories in the East and Midwest. Among the many objects made were pressed pin, powder and candy boxes. They come in many different patterns, and it would be possible to build a very substantial collection by confining oneself to this medium alone.

Interest in glass containers continued to increase. During the 1920s manufacturers turned out cigarette and cigar boxes in the prevailing Art Deco mode, often combining glass with such metals as silver, stainless steel, chrome or pewter. The craze for carnival glass (so named because cheaper versions were often given away as prizes at fairs and carnivals) was at its height about the same time. This gaudy, iridescent glass appeared in many forms, including tobacco and various dresser boxes. Now it is once more avidly collected.

By the 1930s carnival glass had been replaced by an even cheaper mass-produced type known appropriately enough as Depression glass. This, too, was utilized in making containers, primarily those intended for the kitchen and for use at table.

Plastics in some form have been available ever since 1862, when Alexander Parkes of Birmingham, England, invented Parkesine. Various problems, including their high flammability, limited the use of early plastics until the invention of Celluloid in 1871. This substance was widely used in Victorian dresser sets and jewelry boxes.

In 1910 the U.S. Bakelite Corporation was founded to produce Bakelite, another plastic that had been developed three years before by a Belgian physicist. Bakelite could be made in a range of colors. During the period 1920 to 1950 it was used in numerous Art Deco containers, including cigarette and vanity cases, jewelry and tobacco boxes—pieces that are readily available and widely collected today. Various urea- and vinyl-based plastics replaced Bakelite in the 1950s; no doubt boxes of these substances will also become collectible in time.

Canada and the United States have been culturally integrated to a great extent for many years, so that most box types and materials produced in one nation will be found in the other. A notable exception, of course, is the distinctly French decoration found on earlier containers made in the province of Quebec.

Eskimo Culture Interesting and artistically appealing containers have been produced by the Eskimo, or Inuit, as they prefer to be called. This hardy people lives along the Arctic shores from Greenland west across Canada to Alaska and the islands of the Bering Sea. Organized loosely into family groups, the Eskimo have survived and even thrived under difficult conditions for thousands of years. The overwhelming majority of their existent boxes, however, date to the so-called historic period, which began in 1750 with the first contacts with white culture.

Since almost all Eskimo were originally nomadic, the containers they made were composed of whatever materials were available at a given time and place. Ivory, wood, basketry materials, leather and even stone have been called into play.

The carving of ivory appears always to have had significance for Eskimo artisans. The work was traditionally limited to males, and the objects produced—hunting amulets and effigy figures, for example—were often believed to possess supernatural powers. Small wonder then that so much skill and effort were expended even on household objects.

The ivory utilized in such work was obtained from several sources. Until well into the nineteenth century, much of it was the dark yellow material known as "old ivory"—the tusks of prehistoric mammoths, which had been preserved in the perpetually frozen

89.
Snuffbox, carved ivory bound in leather and bark. Once they had made contact with the whites, the Eskimo became snuff takers and produced containers for the substance. Eskimo, Alaskan, Point Hope, late nineteenth to early twentieth century. Height: 8.9 cm. (3½ in.). Museum of the American Indian, New York, Heye Foundation

90

91

90.
Needlecase, ivory, carved and incised. The importance of the seal and walrus to the Eskimo economy is reflected in the many objects on which these animals are depicted. Eskimo, Alaskan, late nineteenth to early twentieth century. Length: 15 cm. (6 in.). Smithsonian Institution, National Museum of Natural History

91.
Oval box, probably for tools, carved and incised wood with ivory handle and decorative elements. Although generally hard to come by, wood was used by the Eskimo in box manufacture. Eskimo, Alaskan, Cape Prince of Wales, late nineteenth to early twentieth century. Length: 15.2 cm. (6 in.). Museum of the American Indian, New York, Heye Foundation, Judge Nathan Bijur Collection

Colorplate 26.
Storage box, carved and painted cedar wood. The bear on this Haida box is represented in a style common to a number of tribes of the Northwest Coast. American Indian, Haida, British Columbia, nineteenth century. Length: 46 cm. (18⅛ in.). Smithsonian Institution, National Museum of Natural History

soil. This was supplemented by ivory picked up along the coast where walrus had died. Finally, of course, there were tusks acquired from walrus killed on the hunt.

Since ivory was always valuable, containers shaped out of it tend to be relatively small. Snuffboxes (plate 89) are a popular item. Designed to contain a mixture of tobacco and fungus ash, they were generally a few inches high, circular and frequently adorned with a lifelike representation of a seal or walrus head. The seal and the walrus that were so important to Eskimo life are often depicted as decorative elements on Eskimo boxes. Needlecases (plate 90) and the containers for game counters might be carved in the likeness of these animals. More usually, though, the top and sides would be decorated with the incised designs we have come to associate with Eskimo art.

These decorations have traditionally been connected with the life of the Inuit, and typically show the people at work skinning seals or building homes, hunting across the ice or taking part in dances and rituals. The earliest examples of such work, known among collectors as "old-style engraving," are characterized by a minimal attention to detail, sticklike figures and the introduction into the engraved lines of ash mixed with oil, or less often red ocher similarly treated. In each case, the coloring agent tends to emphasize the design.

After 1870, partly as a result of the contact with whalers and other outsiders, Eskimo craftsmen began to create larger panoramas, often using a whole walrus tusk for a single drawing, or covering the entire side of a box with a scene. At the same time the characters portrayed became larger and more lifelike, and shading and contrast increased.

This "modified style of engraving," as it is known, was utilized until about 1900, when a Western pictorial style was introduced, resulting in an almost photographic representation of Eskimo life and wildlife. Most carving and engraving available to collectors today dates from this last period. Since World War II, engraving has declined because of the restrictions on the use of ivory, and Inuit craftsmen have generally turned to carving soapstone instead.

Wood was often hard to come by, especially for the Inuit in more northern areas, but it was always an important material. Smaller boxes might be hollowed and shaped from a single large block of timber; but in most cases the size of the piece of wood available prohibited such a course. Containers were far more likely to be pieced together from small bits of driftwood, with wooden pegs or leather thongs being used to join the individual units.

Some surprisingly fine examples have been made this way. Particularly appealing are the oval toolboxes with domed lids that are used to store everything from harpoon heads to modern steel-bladed knives. These boxes are often decorated with pieces of carved ivory (fish, seals and the like), which are attached to the surface with pegs or tiny pieces of leather (plate 91).

Other examples in wood include sewing boxes made for the women of the tribe, inlaid or otherwise embellished with ivory, and small tobacco boxes used to safeguard precious chewing tobacco. Like snuffs and some storage boxes, these containers may be carved in the form of a whale, otter, seal or walrus.

Twigs and grass or rushes have been used for containers, as has woven or beaten leather. Most such examples are made by women for purely utilitarian purposes and are not particularly attractive. Nevertheless, for the serious collector they represent an important aspect of the Inuit craft.

Indian Culture A far greater range of containers has been produced by the many tribes of Indians inhabiting North America from Canada down to as far south as the Mexican border. Indeed, the boxes made by these peoples are as varied as the Indians themselves.

From the Northwest Coastal tribes, whose domain once stretched from Alaska south to British Columbia, come remarkable carved boxes and chests in which food and clothing were stored (colorplate 26). The Haida, Tlingit, Tsimshian and Kwakiutl tribes are regarded as the finest wood carvers produced by the Americas, and among the world's best. Employing the great stands of spruce and cedar native to the region, they turned out containers that combined striking sculptural forms with surfaces skillfully painted and frequently inlaid with abalone shell.

In the potlatch, the ceremony of ritual impoverishment during which an individual or an entire family gave large gifts to others, ostensibly to show their disdain for wealth, Coastal boxes were a favorite offering. As a result, many of these wonderful containers were burned or cast into the sea. The ones that survive, along with similarly made totem poles and dance masks, indicate the great sophistication of the carvers.

The finer examples are often made of one or two pieces of wood bent to shape and pegged together, then decorated either with incised work or light carving. Once the carving was completed, the forms would be painted and the abalone pieces inlaid. Decorative motifs consist primarily of abstract renditions of deities, animals and people related to the history of a given tribe or a particular family. Certain characters, such as the bear, the owl, the raven and the killer whale, appear over and over again in designs from various tribes. But they are treated in so highly stylized a manner that it is often difficult to recognize a specific creature unless one is familiar with the carving style involved.

The Northwestern Coastal tribes were masters of the difficult art of fitting decorative designs into a specific form or area, and they

92.
Covered container, woven of maidenhair fern and bear grass dyed with lichen. The tribes native to California have produced some of the world's finest basketry. The shape of this basket is found only among the Karok. American Indian, Karok, California, c. 1900–1920. Height: 8.9 cm. (3½ in.). Museum of the American Indian, New York, Heye Foundation, gift of Mrs. Thea Heye

utilized their skill in making containers from other materials in addition to wood. Chief among these were copper, which was obtained primarily from traders, horn (colorplate 27), ivory and basketry. Coastal containers in copper are often rather small and on the whole uncommon; tinder- and snuffboxes are the usual forms. Ivory was employed for similar objects, as well as for the needle- and sewing cases utilized by women.

Ivory from this region was decorated and carved just as it was by the Eskimo; but the Coastal examples tend to be embellished with designs that are more intricate and more closely related to the form of the object than is the case farther north. Basketry woven containers generally were made from cedar bark, which was shredded and then woven into fibers. Natural dyes were used to stain the decorative patterns, and the whole process, while lengthy, resulted in very fine, often watertight pieces.

Farther south along the coast dwelt the so-called California tribes, small groups of foragers and subsistence farmers who were largely wiped out by the whites following the Gold Rush of the 1850s. Although they lived quite simply, these peoples, who included the Hupa, the Klamath and particularly the Pomo, are generally regarded as the finest basket makers the world has ever seen. Utilizing everything from ferns and lichens to split roots and bird feathers, they created boxes (plate 92) and baskets of extraordinary delicacy. Some are less than two inches in diameter, and all are decorated with bold, geometric designs. Early California basketry today brings prices to rival those paid for Egyptian and ancient European examples.

The many tribes of the southwestern United States occupied a semi-arid environment where basketry was less important than pottery making. Sun-baked or dung-fired vessels from this region were decorated with vivid designs of a predominantly geometric form. Most examples were jars or ollas, but a few round or square boxes will be found.

To the north and east of these peoples dwelt the Plains Indians, free-roaming horsemen who were roughly divided into northern, central and southern groups. Almost constantly on the move, they had little use for basketry or ceramics; but they developed the art of beadwork decoration and utilized the hide of the buffalo they hunted in making such items as whetstone cases and parfleche storage boxes. The latter were frequently decorated with painted scenes of domesticity or warfare.

The more sedentary tribes of the Midwest, such as the Chippewa and the Kickapoo, created containers of bark, bent and bound together with twig or leather thongs. These were often decorated with figures of humans and animals that might be incised into the surface or left to stand out when surrounding areas of the bark (usually birch) were scraped away. Midwestern Indians were also skilled in the working

93.
Rectangular covered container, splint with polychrome paint. Basketry containers are still made by various tribes, although today they are produced primarily as commercial goods. American Indian, Mohegan, New Haven, Connecticut, 1860–70. Length: 27.3 cm. (10¾ in.). Museum of the American Indian, New York, Heye Foundation

94.
Oblong covered storage box, birch bark sewn together with roots and decorated by scraping through one layer of bark to the next. American Indian, Passamaquoddy, Maine, early twentieth century. Length: 24.8 cm. (9¾ in.). Museum of the American Indian, New York, Heye Foundation

95.
Box containing an eagle-feather headdress, wood with an incised pictographic song record. The midwestern tribes carved a variety of objects from such woods as pine, birch and maple. American Indian, Chippewa, Wisconsin, late nineteenth century. Length: 23.5 cm. (9¼ in.). Museum of the American Indian, New York, Heye Foundation

of wood. Their boxes (plate 95), like their bowls and some utensils, were made out of beech and maple (among other woods), which were polished to a high gloss and frequently inlaid with bone or the shell of the freshwater mussel.

Once whites became dominant in the area, the older crafts faded away. But the tribes continued to practice certain popular arts such as beadwork, and beaded cigarette and card cases were turned out for the tourist trade. This craft proved especially lucrative for the northern and midwestern tribes, among whom it is still practiced.

From existent artifacts, it is evident that the tribes of the American Southeast, such as the Creek and the Natchez, were among the finest of North American craftsmen. Burial sites have revealed bone and shell containers decorated with incised geometric designs and inlaid in contrasting materials, while pottery finds have included large boxes and urns with elaborate appliqué work. The tribes of the Northeast, where the great Iroquois confederacy opposed the Algonquin peoples of New England and Canada, were almost equally creative. The Iroquois are perhaps best known for their grotesque dance masks; the Algonquin produced a variety of other craft objects, including splint boxes (plate 93), which were usually decorated free hand or block-

93

Colorplate 27.
Cylindrical covered box, carved horn inlaid with haliotis shell. The carving represents a bear. North American Indian, Tlingit, Alaska, c. 1920. Height: 8.9 cm. (3½ in.). Museum of the American Indian, New York, Heye Foundation

94

95

printed with patterns in so-called potato stamp decoration, and birch-bark containers (plate 94).

They also shaped wood, transforming it into everything from burl bowls and eating utensils to unusual boat-shaped fetish boxes in which sacred spirits might reside. These containers were often covered with cross hatching and complex geometric designs.

To store maple sugar, the Iroquois made vessels of birch bark, and to hold their personal items they made small containers shaped from porcupine quills, which were dyed in various hues, then sewn to a bark or woven grass background. Quillwork is an ancient Indian art that is still practiced in the East and Midwest for commercial reasons, although on the Plains it has been largely superseded by beadwork.

Finally, the Micmac of Nova Scotia should be mentioned for their dyed quillwork (colorplate 28). Another, even more esoteric Indian skill comes from New England and Canada: that of weaving moose hair into a subtle appliqué used to enliven such mundane objects as cigar and cigarette containers (plate 96).

South America In terms of social organization and land controlled, the Indians of North America cannot, of course, be compared to the indigenous peoples of Central and South America. Three great cultures—the Aztec, Inca and Maya—produced centrally organized societies, vast cities and a veritable wealth of artistic and craft objects, the great bulk of which was destroyed during the European conquest of the fifteenth and sixteenth centuries.

What remains, though (primarily in the fields of pottery, stone and metalwork), indicates a high level of achievement. In Mexico, the stone-working Olmec were established as early as 1000 B.C.; and they were followed by the Toltec, the Maya and the Aztec. The last arose farther south, but by 1200 they had spread north into Mexico, where some of the most interesting remains have been found. The Aztecs made objects of shell, bone and stone, and shaped square or rectangular covered boxes decorated with raised figures and complex stylized forms (plate 97).

The area that is now Costa Rica was home to the Chorotega and the Nicarao, both masters of the ceramic arts. The Chorotega produced unusual, sophisticated containers in the form of birds (plate 98), animals and humans; both groups turned out work in gold, including small boxlike containers of various sorts whose purposes we can often only guess at.

In South America important cultural groups can be traced back for 10,000 years. In 900–500 B.C. the Chavin were producing excellent figures and containers in gold, as well as bright polychrome pottery. A related group, the Mochica (250 B.C.–A.D. 750), were also potters. They were succeeded by the Chimú (A.D. 1000–1500), who

96

Colorplate 28.
Covered storage box, dyed porcupine quills over a birch-bark core. Quillwork is a complex and demanding art form. American Indian, Micmac, Nova Scotia, c. 1900. Height: 10.2 cm. (4 in.). Museum of the American Indian, New York, Heye Foundation

96.
Cigar box, birch bark decorated with moose-hair appliqué. Moose-hair appliqué work was used to ornament utilitarian objects as well as clothing. American Indian, Huron, Quebec, Canada, 1850–75. Height: 14.6 cm. (5¾ in.). Museum of the American Indian, New York, Heye Foundation

established a great center at Chan Chan with a population of over 100,000. The Chimú worked in gold, copper, ceramics and textiles. Their wooden boxes, embellished with incised images, included stylized representations of animals (plate 99).

There can be no doubt that the artistic output of all these societies was immense. However, so much has been lost or deliberately destroyed that boxes from the region, like most other artifacts, are very rare today.

Once the European culture was established, new forms began to emerge. The Spanish and the Portuguese built their churches and then proceeded to train native craftsmen in Western techniques and design to provide the large number of decorative and ritual items required. In common with other items from the colonial era, boxes and containers of this time often reflect a curious blend of Indian craftsmanship and European motifs.

At a later period most pieces became almost completely European in feeling, and substantial quantities, dating from the eighteenth through the early twentieth centuries, can still be obtained. They include boxes in silver and copper, ceramic containers and those made of polychromed wood, leather and glass. Due to the shortage of earlier, native forms, collectors have to be content with these.

It should be mentioned, though, that in certain regions, notably Mexico and Bolivia, Indian crafts have survived in a modified form. There appealing containers in pottery, wood (plate 100) and basketry materials may still be found.

97.
Box, carved stone decorated with various stylized designs. Some of the Aztec stone carvings are of great size, but this box is only slightly more than a foot wide. Aztec, Middle American, c. 1500. Width: 33 cm. (13 in.). Museum of the American Indian, New York, Heye Foundation

98.
Two-piece container in the form of a harpy eagle, baked clay. The Central and South American peoples were skilled potters, and have left behind many fine ceramic objects. Central American, Chorotega culture, Costa Rica, Guanacaste, c. 900–1500. Height: 21.6 cm. (8½ in.). Museum of the American Indian, New York, Heye Foundation

97

99.
Carved wooden box with cover, incised decoration. It is unusual to find a wooden object of this age so well preserved. South American, Chimú culture, Peru, Trujillo, c. 900–1200. Length: 23.5 cm. (9¼ in.). Museum of the American Indian, New York, Heye Foundation

100.
Cylindrical box with conical cover, wood carved and painted. Containers such as these were frequently used to carry anything from tobacco to foodstuffs. South American, probably Brazil's Amazon Valley, nineteenth century. Height: 36.8 cm. (14½ in.). Museum of the American Indian, New York, Heye Foundation

98

100

99

Just one more.

7 Advice for Collectors

The box collector, unlike enthusiasts in some other areas of antiques, is presented with an appealing variety; moreover, pieces on the market are often relatively inexpensive. For many collectors, the major problem is how to know when to stop—to limit their collections in order to retain both storage space and sufficient display space.

New collectors generally do best by concentrating on containers made from a particular material, mother-of-pearl, say, or silver, or on a specific type of box, snuffs or card cases or matchsafes (colorplate 29). In this way the collection achieves coherent form and the collector is usually able to learn much more about his or her acquisitions.

Learning is important from both a practical and an aesthetic point of view. The knowledgeable collector will be able to spot rarities, distinguish fakes or heavily repaired pieces and recognize underpriced examples. Furthermore, knowing about the history, construction and place of origin of your treasures will greatly enhance your pleasure in collecting.

But for the beginner, particularly, it is often difficult to settle on an area for study. Fortunately, the nature of boxes allows for interesting choices. You might decide to collect on the basis of material or perhaps on the basis of shape. Certain shapes reappear frequently; at the most obvious level, you could accumulate square, round, or even triangular boxes. Much more interesting, though, is the collection of highly specific shapes. It is quite possible to amass a sizable collection of containers in the shape of hearts, flowers, stars, shoes or even hats. Many similar categories exist, each providing an exciting structure for the field.

Or you might choose to collect along national lines, trying to acquire as many different boxes as possible from, say, France or

Colorplate 29.
A group of matchsafes in various materials. Matchsafes came in a wide variety of forms and were popular accessories of dress during the Victorian era. English and American, late nineteenth to twentieth century. Cooper-Hewitt Museum, gift of Carol B. Brener and Stephen W. Brener

China. Such an approach can be generalized or confined to specifics: African wooden boxes, for example. The possibilities of this approach are almost unlimited.

For the historically minded, there is yet another approach. Over the years containers have been associated with historic personages and events, either because the boxes themselves were involved—a snuffbox given to a loyal follower by an Italian duke—or because the container commemorates a specific event. Examples of the former sort are hard to locate and frequently costly; but large numbers of mementos exist. The English still make small porcelain boxes to celebrate, say, the coronation of a new king or queen, and American containers in tin, glass, wood and pottery have been created to mark such events as the Centennial of 1876 and Bicentennial of 1976 and the various world's fairs.

The Reading and Reference section (page 123) will provide a variety of sources for both general and specialized knowledge of the field, and periodic visits to museums, many of which are listed under Public Collections (page 124), will enable the enthusiast to master a variety of box forms. Antiques shops and shows can provide further pointers, as well as give an idea of current prices in the field.

Knowledge breeds refinement. The knowledgeable collector in almost every case comes to seek out only the highest quality obtainable within budget limitations. This is prudent not only because it is always nice to have fine things but also because in every area of antiques, experience has shown that the better-quality items appreciate more rapidly in good times and depreciate less in a declining economy.

The more you know, the more likely you are to spot the rare or valuable piece, hopefully at a price well below its true worth. However, if you doubt your knowledge, then by all means deal only with antiques dealers who come well recommended and will guarantee their wares. While fakes and reproductions are less of a problem in this field than some others, it is still possible to get fooled. The lovely lapped wooden boxes originally made by Shaker craftsmen are now widely reproduced—often with remarkable accuracy. Since the nineteenth-century containers sell for $200 or $300 apiece, a mistake can be costly. Again, many African boxes are of quite recent vintage; one must know this, or deal with someone reliable who does.

Among European and Oriental containers, the problem of reproduction may be compounded by restoration. A two-hundred-year-old enamel box may have been chipped, an ancient ivory snuff may have lost a piece or two along the way. Skilled artisans can disguise such deficiencies with repairs that are hard to detect. The more you know about how the pieces were made, the more likely you are to recognize such work. Technical aids such as the black light, a fluorescent light that can reveal overpainting and repairs to pottery, may assist the detective work, but in the final analysis a collector's knowledge provides the best protection.

This is not to say that one should never buy a repaired box. If you are seeking rarities, it may be impossible otherwise to obtain what you want. But you should always pay less for restored examples, and wherever possible they are to be avoided.

The relative abundance of boxes makes the question of where to find them a simple one. Unless you choose to collect very early examples or ones made from precious materials, it is possible to find boxes virtually everywhere. Later examples show up at almost every yard sale and flea market. For better quality there are antiques shops and shows, and if you have become highly specialized, it is always possible to advertise your wants—either in the numerous trade papers or in your hometown newspaper. Some surprising bargains surface when one begins to advertise.

Once all these wonderful things accumulate, it becomes necessary to preserve, store and display them. Preservation can be particularly important. Since boxes are made of so many different materials, you should know something about the protection and conservation of everything from silver to papier-mâché. Fortunately, good books on conservation are readily available.

Storage is seldom a problem since most boxes are small; they should, however, be individually wrapped and packed. Display, of course, is very much a personal matter. Everything from a table top to rows of custom-made, individually lighted shelves can serve to show off these appealing collectibles.

Glossary

applied decoration, a separately formed decorative element attached to the surface of an object.

Battersea boxes, enamel boxes that were made at York House in Battersea between 1753 and 1756; generally decorated with transfer-printed or painted designs.
bible box, a small carved chest used to store books and other objects.
boulle, marquetry of brass and tortoiseshell, usually inlaid.
bride's box, a large, generally oval or round box; a traditional wedding gift for a bride, particularly in the Germanic countries and in the Pennsylvania area in the United States.
bright cut, in silver work, a type of deeply engraved decoration that uses geometric lines to create a brilliant effect.

candle box, a hanging wall box with sloping lid used to store candles.
chip carving, decorative carving produced by gouging tiny triangular chips from a wood surface with a chisel or a knife. Also called *notch* or *gouge carving*.
cloisonné, the technique of covering the surface of a piece of metal with a design produced by brushing powdered enamel into areas separated by small brass walls (cloisons), and then heating the object to melt and fuse the enamel.
coffer, a small strongbox used to store valuables; often iron-bound.
comfit box, a small container that originally held comfits, or bits of nuts, candied fruits, or seeds.

damascening, the art of inlaying gold or silver wire into a steel, iron or bronze surface.
decoupage, the art of decorating a surface by applying to it cutouts, usually of paper, and then covering them with varnish or lacquer.

emboss, to make raised designs on the surface of a piece of leather, metal or paper, often through use of a press.
enamel, a glasslike substance that is fused to a metal base under heat.
engine turning, a technique for creating surface designs on metal or pottery by cutting into the surface while the piece turns on a lathe.
engrave, to produce designs on the surface of a piece of metal by incising or cutting into the surface with small, sharp tools.
étui, a small ornamental case or box that held a woman's personal articles such as needles, thimbles and small scissors.

faience, the French term for tin-glazed earthenware; also an archaeological term for ancient Egyptian glazed powdered quartz wares.
filigree work, use of fine silver or gold wire either to create openwork objects or to decorate solid pieces of metal.

gesso, a mixture of plaster and water used to coat the surface of wood or canvas before painting.
gilding, the application of gold leaf or a similar substance to a wood, metal, ceramic or leather surface.
gouache, the art of painting with pigments that have been tempered by gum mixed with pipe clay and water.
ground, the dominant background color in a decorated piece of pottery, wood, etc.

Imari, a Japanese export porcelain usually decorated with rich, colorful underglaze designs; manufactured in Arita, beginning in about 1700.
incense box, a type of small generally round or square box used in the Orient to store incense.
incising, the technique of producing designs by cutting into a surface.
inlay, to employ a decorative technique involving sinking materials of contrasting color or nature into areas cut in a solid surface.
inro, a small compartmented box, usually of lacquer, worn on a cord by the Japanese, whose clothing had no pockets.

japanning, the technique of imitating lacquerwork by applying several coats of varnish to a surface, then baking the object in an oven.

lacquer, colored varnish made from the sap of the lac tree, *Rhus verniciflua*.

marbleizing, the technique of applying colors to a surface in imitation of marble.
marquetry, a type of veneered surface achieved by glueing thin pieces of shaped wood to a solid surface in various patterns.
matchsafe, a protective container for carrying matches; first manufactured in the nineteenth century, and popular until safety matches and lighters came into vogue.
mosaic work, the inlaying of stone, ceramic or glass fragments into a solid ground.

nécessaire, the French term for a small compartmented casket or container used to store toothpicks, cutlery, sewing utensils or shaving articles.
niello, a black substance composed of powdered silver and other materials, used as a filling for incised decoration on silver.

parcel gilding, the application of gold to only a portion of an object, usually one of silver or bronze.
pastiglia, a molded paste used to decorate boxes in Renaissance Italy, probably in an attempt to give the impression of a more expensive metal box.
patch box, a small box made of various materials and used to hold small pieces of silk or taffeta that were glued onto the face to cover scars left by smallpox.
pâte-de-verre, a ground and molded glass, which often has the appearance of precious and semiprecious stones.
pewter, an alloy of tin and lead, usually with copper or antimony added.
pillbox, a small box used to carry pills or other medicines.
pyxides, small cylindrical, covered vessels, used in classical Greece and Rome to hold salves and toiletries. The singular is *pyxis*.

reliquary, a small container in which sacred objects are stored.
reserve, in ceramic decoration, that area of the surface which is surrounded by a border and contains an enclosed design.
rosemaling, a popular Scandinavian painted floral decoration used on boxes, furniture, and other woodwork.

salt box, a container, usually of wood but sometimes of metal or pottery, used to store salt.
scrimshaw, incised decoration on bone, usually ivory.
seal box, a small box designed to hold royal seals.
shagreen, sharkskin, popular since the eighteenth century as a durable, waterproof covering for boxes, tea caddies, and other containers and receptacles.
soap box, an oval box, often of silver, which was part of the toilet set and served to store a piece of soap.
spongework, the application of irregular, splotchy color, often with a sponge, to a ground of contrasting color.
straw-work, ornamentation consisting of small pieces of straw, bleached or colored, and arranged in patterns to ornament boxes and other small objects.

tea caddy, a box used to hold tea.
tobacco box, an oval box, often in brass or silver, used to store loose tobacco. Larger than a snuffbox.
toleware, wares of japanned tin, most commonly with black, yellow, red, or green grounds and bold peasant decoration.
Tunbridge ware, small wooden objects, made primarily at Tunbridge Wells in England, which are decorated with a kind of marquetry or mosaic pattern made by applying cross sections cut from rods of different colored woods glued together in various patterns to form a mosaic.

veneering, the application of thin strips of rare or expensive wood to the surface of a piece made of more ordinary wood.
vertu, a term used for small items in various metals, such as étuis and snuffboxes.
vinaigrette, a small box of gold or silver used to carry a perfumed sponge, which could be sniffed to cover up unpleasant odors.

workbox, a fitted box, customarily of wood, employed by seamstresses to store needles, threads and the like.

Reading and Reference

General

Blakemore, Kenneth. *Snuff Boxes*. London: Frederick Muller, 1974.
Chu, Arthur and Grace. *Oriental Antiques and Collectibles, A Guide*. New York: Crown Publishers, 1973.
DeLieb, Eric. *Silver Boxes*. New York: Exeter Books, 1979.
DeSager, Eric, and Kenneth Blakemore. *Antiques*. London: Octopus Books, 1978.
Harrison, Hazel, ed. *World Antiques*. Secaucus, N.J.: Chartwell Books, 1978.
Klamkin, Marian. *The Collector's Book of Boxes*. New York: Dodd, Mead, 1970.
Latham, Jean. *Collecting Miniature Antiques*. New York: Charles Scribner's Sons, 1972.
Mackay, James. *An Encyclopedia of Small Antiques*. New York: Harper & Row, 1975.
Perry, Evan. *Collecting Antique Metalware*. Garden City, N.Y.: Doubleday, 1974.
Pinto, Edward H. *Treen or Small Woodenware Throughout the Ages*. London: B. T. Batsford, 1949.
Pushkavior, V., ed. *Russian Applied Arts*. Leningrad: Aurora Art Publishers, 1976.

American

Carlisle, Lilian Baker. *Hat Boxes and Bandboxes at the Shelburne Museum*. Shelburne, Vt.: The Shelburne Museum, 1960.
Goulde, Mary Earle. *Early American Woodenware*. Rev. ed., Springfield, Mass.: The Pond-Ekberg Co., 1948.
Ketchum, William C. *American Basketry and Woodenware*. New York: Macmillan Publishing Co., 1974.
Little, Nina Fletcher. *Neat and Tidy, Boxes and Their Contents*. New York: E. P. Dutton, 1980.

Some Public Collections of Boxes

UNITED STATES

Chicago: The Art Institute of Chicago
Minneapolis: The Minneapolis Institute of Arts
New York City: The American Museum of Natural History
The Brooklyn Museum
Cooper-Hewitt Museum,
the Smithsonian Institution's National Museum of Design
The Metropolitan Museum of Art
Museum of American Folk Art
Museum of the American Indian
Philadelphia: Philadelphia Museum of Art
The University Museum
Pittsfield, Mass.: Hancock Shaker Village, Shaker Community, Inc.
Washington, D.C.: Smithsonian Institution
Freer Gallery of Art
National Museum of American History

OTHER

Berlin: Kunstgewerbemuseum
Delft: Stedelijk Museum
Istanbul: Topkapi Sarayi Müzesi
Leningrad: State Hermitage Museum
London: Victoria and Albert Museum
Paris: Musée des Arts Décoratifs
Stockholm: Nationalmuseum
Taipei: The National Palace Museum
Tokyo: The Tokyo National Museum
Vienna: Kunsthistorisches Museum

Index

Numbers in *italics* indicate pages on which black-and-white illustrations appear. Numbers in **boldface** indicate pages on which colorplates appear.

Acknowledgments

Cooper-Hewitt staff members have been responsible for the following contributions to the series: concept, Lisa Taylor; administration, Christian Rohlfing, Peter Scherer and Kurt Struver. In addition, valuable help has been provided by S. Dillon Ripley, Joseph Bonsignore, Susan Hamilton and Robert W. Mason of the Smithsonian Institution, as well as by Gloria Norris, Edward E. Fitzgerald, Madeleine Karter, Neal Jones and the late Warren Lynch of Book-of-the-Month Club, Inc.

The author wishes to thank the following for their kind assistance: Nancy Akre, whose encouragement and advice greatly facilitated preparation of the book; Dorothy Sinha, who patiently sought out photographs; Rosemary Corroon, who assisted in the selection of objects for inclusion in the book; David McFadden and Christian Rohlfing, whose comments on the text were of great help; and Neal Jones and Ann Adelman.

Credits

Courtesy of the Brooklyn Museum: plates 52, 53, 55, 57; color 2, 16. Cooper-Hewitt Museum: plate 43, color 29 (T. K. Rose, photographer); plates 3–6, 10–17, 19, 22–24, 26–28, 30–35, 37, 38, 42, 44, 47, 58, 60, 65–69, 72, 77, 78, 86, color 4–10, 20, 25 (Scott Hyde, photographer); color 24; *endpapers;* page 121. The *Forbes* Magazine Collection, New York (H. Peter Curran, photographer): color 11. Courtesy of the Freer Gallery of Art, Smithsonian Institution, Washington, D.C.: color 18, 19, 21. Hancock Shaker Village/Shaker Community, Inc., Pittsfield, Massachusetts (photographer, Paul J. Rocheleau): plate 82. The Metropolitan Museum of Art: plates 1, 2, 20, 25, 29, 36, 41, 45, 46, 48–51, 54, 56, 59, 61–64, 70, 71, 73–76, 79, 80, 83; color *frontispiece* and color 1, 3, 12–14, 17. The Minneapolis Institute of Arts: plates 7, 8. Collection du Musée des Arts Décoratifs, Paris: plates 18, 21 (photographer, L. Sully-Jaulmes). Museum of American Folk Art, New York: color 22, 23 (Helga Photo Studio, Inc.). Courtesy of the Museum of the American Indian, Heye Foundation, New York: plates 89, 91–100; color 27, 28. Private collection: plates 81, 84, 85, 87, 88. Smithsonian Institution, National Museum of American History: plates 39, 40. Smithsonian Institution, National Museum of Natural History: plate 90; color 26. University Museum, University of Pennsylvania: color 15. Victoria and Albert Museum, London: plate 9.

DESIGN ASSOCIATE: Laurie Rippon

PUTNAM
AND ROFF. PAPER
HANGING &
MANUFAC
BOX
BAND
HARTFORD
CON

PUTNAM
AND ROFF. PAPER
HANGING &
MANUFAC
BOX
BAND
HARTFORD
CON